FINANCIAL ADVISOR SECRETS OF SUCCESS

TIPS, TOOLS AND RESOURCES FOR

BECOMING A SUCCESSFUL

FINANCIAL ADVISOR

MICHAEL D. DUNIGAN

Ordering Information:
Quantity sales. Special discounts are available on quantity purchases by corporations, associations, and others. For details, contact the publisher at the email address above.
Orders by U.S. trade bookstores and wholesalers. Please contact 828 Publishing or visit www.financialadvisorapp.com.

978-1-7357694-0-0
978-1-7357694-1-7
978-1-7357694-2-4

Printed in the United States of America
1st Edition

Table of Contents

Introduction   7

Chapter 1 - Begin at the Beginning   15

Chapter 2 - Developing Your Plan   29

Chapter 3 - Building Your Network   39

Chapter 4 – Marketing   51

Chapter 5 - Prospects & Meetings   113

Chapter 6 – Conclusion   121

This project of passion is dedicated to my three boys:
Riley, Lucas & Breck

"Always Finish What You Start"

INTRODUCTION

"The divine insanity of noble minds, that never falters nor abates, but labors, endures, and waits, till all that it foresees it finds, or what cannot find, creates."

—LONGFELLOW

There are many reasons why I chose to become a financial advisor. Personally, I find great satisfaction in helping people achieve financial success. Professionally, this is a career that incorporates a lot of my strengths: I'm good with numbers and people, I pay attention to detail, and I can relate to various personalities while establishing trust and commonality. This career also allows for a lot of creative flexibility, which I enjoy.

The first year in this business is extremely difficult. Shoot, the first three years are difficult. This is a career that requires adaptability, determination, and endless drive. This is not a career where you should have a backup plan—you must commit yourself to being successful every single day. By following the advice in this book and giving 100% effort, the likelihood of you successfully navigating your first few years as a financial advisor increases tremendously.

Early in my career I was frustrated by the lack of information or guidance available on how to survive the first few years as a financial advisor. I was told to make phone calls, call my friends & family, and knock on doors. To a certain extent this is true but was lacking a couple critical components: PREPERATION & FOCUS. An activity is just an activity; by itself there can be no long-term success. However, if you prepare and focus your activities toward a specific target, success will follow.

Let's use hunting a deer as an example. After waking up around 9 in the morning, I throw a rifle and some ammo in my truck, drive out to the woods and start walking around looking for a deer. What do you think is the chance of me finding a mature buck to bring home? I would agree – pretty low.

Now, we're going to run this scenario again, but this time we're going to do some prior preparation and research. The sound and light of my alarm cuts the darkness of the room and my sleep. After about 20 minutes of groggy fumbling, I'm packing up my truck. Steam from my coffee fogs the windshield as the motor turns over. 45 minutes later, the crunch and crackle under my tires slowly stops as I pull to the edge of the gravel road. The sun is mere moments from peaking over the horizon as I shoulder my Winchester rifle over my arm and begin the 12-minute hike toward Ripple Creek.

Feeling fresh and excited, I spot recent tracks, and make my way about 40 yards into the thicket to set up my camouflaged spot. With a decent view of the path and creek, I wait patiently for my opportunity.

I would say that this second scenario greatly increases my chances of success. My opportunity for success is practically guaranteed if I focus on repeating the same process day after day. Much like this scenario, to be a successful financial advisor you must have the right tools, appropriate knowledge, and a plan for success. Once implemented, conduct your marketing activities on a consistent basis; this produces reliable success time after time.

Now that you are a financial advisor, you have an incredible amount of knowledge and all you need to do is find people who will pay for your expertise. This is where most firms fail young advisors. While training, studying, and passing your examinations can take many months, there is practically no training on the most important aspect of your early career – marketing. Being able to find, connect, and build trust with people to manage their life savings is not a simple task. We're not talking about selling toasters here ladies and gentlemen. We're talking about other people giving you control of their future!

Unfortunately, most training material and books available to you are mostly applicable to advisors who've been in the business for 5+ years. Do you know why? It's because 95% of people who become licensed financial advisors fail out of the business within their first 3 years! This is not a statistic that is shared openly during recruitment and is the driving reason why I chose to write this book. All too often, new advisors mistake activity for achievement. There is only so much time in the day, and you'll be on the clock to produce results or you will be fired. If you spend your time re-writing call scripts, "researching companies", or any number of non-productive activities, then you will quickly find yourself out of time. However, there is one activity, that if done consistently, will help guarantee your success:

MEET AS MANY PEOPLE AS YOU CAN. EVERY DAY.

This sounds so simple. You may be thinking to yourself, *"I love meeting new people. No one can match my drive, knowledge, or passion I have for my career! Once prospects get to know me and trust my knowledge, they will become clients. How could they not?!"* This is a great attitude to have AND a great reason why you will be successful.

But let's pause a moment to think on a few questions...

• How long can I keep up this enthusiasm?

- What happens to my self-talk after 10 unsuccessful meetings?
- How does it feel when a prospect won't return my calls?

Starting a new career or transitioning to a new company is difficult; it is a professional re-birth. This career will chew you up, spit you out, and step on you - if you allow it. At the end of the day we all go home to face our spouse, children, parents ... ourselves. Through it all, you'll be challenged with the emotions all new business owners face: enthusiasm, fear, excitement, self-doubt. This guide is here to alleviate your fears and doubts; to help propel your enthusiasm; to provide you the tools necessary to overcome obstacles and become a successful financial advisor.

It's been said that pain and fear are the greatest motivators—and I agree. When I began my career as a financial advisor, I was excited and enthusiastic, but I was also very fearful. Fearful I'd fail. Fearful I'd say the wrong thing to a prospect. Fearful I'd disappoint my family. It is also said that adversity does not build character, it reveals it. So, take a moment to ask yourself

DO I HAVE THE CHARACTER IT TAKES TO SUCCEED?

Let's reflect on how you felt when you were offered a job as a financial advisor...

- Were you happy?
- Were you nervous?
- Were you excited?
- Have you passed all your examinations? Are you fully licensed?
- How did it feel when you passed your exams? Did you study day and night?
- Was it the fact that you simply passed the tests that made you feel triumphant?
- Or was it that you worked and studied hard; that you never gave up?

If you boil everything down, the single thing you have now is opportunity. You have an opportunity to create a brand, provide life-changing advice, and create a career that is both satisfying and rewarding.

We are not so different from each other. We have similar dreams, hopes, and aspirations; we also have similar fears, doubts, and struggles. Within you is a unique story. It is this story of your life – successes, failures, risks taken (and not taken) that has molded you into the person you are today. It is this human desire to want something more, to be something greater, that gives purpose to our drive. This is your moment, your time. Your opportunity to build a path of success that will carry you the rest of your life!

Commit to your career, give one hundred percent, and you will look back on your first few years as a financial advisor and know that you earned the right to be successful. Trust that the information in this guide will provide you the strong foundation upon which to build a successful financial advisory practice.

CHAPTER 1 - BEGIN AT THE BEGINNING

YOUR GREATEST ASSET

The greatest asset that any one person has is oneself. Your own unique individual talents and skills helps you in all areas of your life: work, home, friends, family, common interactions with others, etc. YOU are the greatest asset to achieving success as a financial advisor. It is imperative that you define your weaknesses and strengths as quickly as possible so that you can improve your weaknesses and practice your strengths. If you are great at analyzing stocks and mutual funds but lousy at starting a conversation with someone, shut down the computer, go to your local supermarket and just start talking to people - talk about anything. Now don't scare anyone, but comment on the prices or products and turn it into a brief dialogue. Make it a point to say hello to everyone you meet throughout the day and ask them how their day is going – be genuine.

A career as a financial advisor can be difficult because your job title is extremely broad. You are an analyst, marketer, teacher, salesperson, therapist, and so much more. It is imperative that you balance these roles to become a well-rounded financial advisor. The one factor that will help you succeed in all these roles is sometimes the toughest to convey to people quickly - trust. As a financial advisor this is the single most important commodity that you must build before providing any services. I believe that this is the toughest hurdle to overcome with people, but once you do the rest is easy.

The financial landscape has changed dramatically over the past thirty years. With the emergence of the internet, on-line banking, trading, and discount brokerage firms have become well known and widely used. People have become more evolved in their search for knowledge because it is more readily available to them. Their hesitancy can be summed up in one phrase, *"Why should I pay this person to do it when I could probably figure it out for myself?"* The answer is that you are a professional who specializes in helping people with their financial lives so that they can have the peace of mind to focus on other things. In order to provide this service to your clients they must trust you.

There was a commercial not long ago for a financial services company that showed a man sitting at his kitchen table with his phone in one hand and a knife in the other. His doctor was on the other end of the phone line saying something like, *"Now make an incision 3 inches above your waist."* The man begins to look nervous and says, *"Shouldn't you be doing this?"* This brief commercial proved a very valid point. Quite a few people think that they know how to invest and can do it themselves, but when faced with the possible consequences of their own personal decisions there is no substitute for professional advice and management.

To be a great financial advisor, it is imperative that you have both a mission statement and a value statement. There is a distinct difference between the two. A mission statement is the goal for your business that helps drive your business model. A value statement is meant to be proclaimed to the world.

MISSION STATEMENT

Your mission statement is a focused idea that directs your practice. This should help to drive your efforts and energy to achieve your short- and long-term goals. Your mission statement should be clear, concise, and encapsulate the primary reason for your practice's existence. A few questions you may ask yourself to formulate your mission statement are:

- Who is my target market?
- What do I provide my clients?
- How will I provide my services?

- What is the goal for my practice?

After you answer these questions it should be easier to formulate a direct mission statement. Once your practice has achieved its goal, the mission statement should be changed to the present tense. The following is an example of a mission statement for a financial advisor:

Through superior client services, outstanding investment analysis, and broad individual solutions XYZ practice will become the most prominent wealth management firm for small business owners and retirees in the mid-west.

VALUE STATEMENT

A value statement is a necessary tool for introducing yourself and your practice. Your value statement should be a clear and concise statement about the value you provide your clients. It should be interesting, differentiate your practice as unique, and leave a person with a clear idea of what you do and what it could mean for them. This is commonly called an elevator speech and should be less than 30 seconds. Here is an example:

As a financial advisor, I work closely with my clients to understand their goals and fears and craft a unique plan to preserve, protect and grow their wealth, minimize taxes, and thoughtfully plan their estate. I love what I do – other than my family, it's what drives me. What about you ... How has this economy affected your family and financial strategy? I'd love to meet over coffee, share some planning strategies, and ultimately compete for your business.

When creating your value statement write down the answers to the following questions.

- Who do I work with?
- Who are my ideal clients?
- What do I help my clients achieve?
- Why is my practice unique?
- How do my client's benefit?

The answers to these questions can help you narrow down the strategic points you want to convey to prospects or other professionals. It is a "mini-commercial" and an opportunity to sell yourself. First impressions are everything in this industry – if you are weak on presenting who you are, what you do, and the value you provide when you first meet a prospect, it is the kiss of death. Therefore, your value statement cannot be too vague or too detailed. It is important to strike the right balance when creating your value statement. Ask friends and coworkers what they think after you have finished, get honest opinions. It is important to memorize your value statement so that it becomes second nature for you and the words just roll off your tongue. While practicing in front of a mirror, stare yourself in the eyes while reciting your statements - this will provide you with the confidence necessary to when introducing yourself and your business to prospects. Memorization also doesn't mean a canned speech, either.

Once you have memorized and internalized anything, you will be able to naturally speak with confidence and personalize so that what you are saying does not come across as forced or pitchy, but with ease.

It is also equally important to follow up your value statement with a call to action. I personally like to engage the person by commenting on a widely known economic issue and ask how they are adapting to it. This creates some doubt in most people's minds. Then I follow up with an offer to meet with me over coffee or lunch. Sometimes, though, I will engage the person and simply hand them my business card and prompt them to visit my website or give me a call.

Think of it this way, if you ask someone else what they do for a living, the only times you truly pay attention is when they are engaging and excited about their work – it's contagious. You need to be the same about your career. Have your value statement memorized, show enthusiasm about your career and engage people with a call to action.

EVERYONE WORKS IN SALES

Ask just about anyone if they would like to be a salesman and nine out of ten times the response will be no. Then ask them what they do for a living and at least some part of their job description will include sales. The very nature of capitalism is to convince other people that they need your services, ideas, or products.

As I was studying to become a financial advisor, I was full of optimism and enthusiasm about the great ways in which I would be helping people and earn a living doing it. Through my expertise, I would be helping people protect their families through insurance planning, craft unique investment portfolios to grow client wealth, create future income through proper retirement planning, and ensure that generations of children would be able to afford college tuition through education planning. The one thing that I did not count on was how stubborn people would be when I offered them my help!

Most people who refused my help fell into one of three categories:

A) They currently worked with a competent advisor.
B) I screwed up the deal (hey, it happens!)
C) They were too comfortable with their status quo.

Too often I would meet with prospects who had a general misconception of their present wants versus future needs. I know that eating loaded nachos and drinking a beer is incrementally detrimental to my long-term health, but I still eat the nachos and drink the beer. How many people smoke a pack of cigarettes a day knowing the long-term health consequences leading to cancer, heart disease, and/or death, but continue to light up anyway? It's the same when it comes to financial planning. Whether it is insurance, investments, retirement, or estate planning I have heard the same excuses (and even used them myself.)

"I can wait a few more months to save for retirement – today I need to buy the latest smart phone. Besides, by then I'll be earning more money and I'll be able to save more."

It is your job as a financial advisor to relate your long-term services in present tense benefits so that your prospects and clients will see the immediate value in working with you. To achieve this, you not only need to be a great financial advisor, but you must be a great salesperson. It is extremely important that you understand that giving advice and being a salesperson are not competing characteristics, but that they complement each other. The most successful financial advisors (and businessmen in general) are the ones with the greatest selling skills. These men and women have learned, practiced, and personalized these skills to match their personality. The best financial advisors do not try to fit themselves into a "mold" of specific sales methods, rather they take those specific sales techniques and match them to their own unique personality. This creates authenticity, conviction, and confidence.

My parents pushed me out the door of the house when I was twelve years old and said that if I wanted to buy my own music, candy, and "stuff" that I would need to get a job. Living in a neighborhood nowhere near a convenience store or any other business, there were no options for employment. My parents offered their help to get me started and suggested that I cut grass. I knocked on the doors of houses in the neighborhood introducing myself and asking if they needed someone to cut their yard. Most said no, but a few said yes. Those that said yes gave me a steady summer job for the next 6 years and a few of those that said no called me from time to time to mow their yard, rake leaves, or do other odd jobs. The second summer of mowing yards, I decided that I wanted to do more to make more money, but mowing grass took a long time and was exhausting. Also, we lived in a large neighborhood and I couldn't possibly push my mower one mile to mow a yard and then push the mower home – it just wasn't cost effective (plainly put – I wasn't doing that!) I talked with my parents and they suggested that I try offering recycling pickup, house-sitting, and pet-sitting. To be effective, my parents taught me that I would have to market differently than I did before.

My father, a successful mortgage broker at the time, gave me one of my first lessons in sales at the young age of twelve. *"Son, for every 100 people you target for your services one or two people will want your help."* He was right. For two weeks I distributed flyers to all the mailboxes in my neighborhood and within three weeks I had lined up quite a few homes to pick up their recycling and also established a great house/pet sitting service for people while they were out of town. My return was about one percent with a few more calling from time to time.

One of the most difficult things that I have had to overcome in my life is why people can't see the same value in products and services that I see. With that eating away at me as a kid distributing flyers and as an adult entering the financial advisory business it used to be hard to except a one to two percent return on marketing efforts. I was finally able to get over this hurdle when I truly began to understand the power in consistency and volume. This is a recurring theme throughout this book and rightfully so. Your future success constantly depends on the work you are doing right now: how many people you are reaching out to and how consistent you are in your efforts. Another hurdle to overcome is how well and for how long you can accept rejection. If you receive a yes approximately one percent of the time than that means for every hundred people you talk to ninety-nine are going to tell you NO. For all your hard work, consistency, and belief in yourself and in your career one of the most important things is to be able to accept no and keep going. Take boxing; this is a high intensity sport that requires strength, muscle, and stamina. Even after months of training and working out every boxer knows that when he or she steps into the ring they are going to get punched. This is a fact. The real choice that the boxer must make is whether to continue fighting after that punch. Just as in boxing, a financial advisor goes through months of training and when it is time to go out and market to your community and bring in new clients, BAM!, you get punched in the face – hopefully not literally, but figuratively. My first few years as a financial advisor I was told "No" day after day. I began doubting my abilities... Did I study long enough? Did I train long enough? Do I even know what I'm doing?" And then ... as if in a whisper, a prospect says "Yes".

It is the most beautiful sound and immediately dismisses all the doubts and fears. In that moment, holding on to that "yes" is all that matters. You want to hold on to it forever, but you must move on to the next "no" because every NO leads you closer to your next YES!

SEEK FIRST...

There's a quote that I've kept with me for many years and it has helped in both my personal and professional life.

"Seek First to Understand, then to be Understood."

This represents a characteristic that can be interpreted, rightfully so, in many great ways. "Seek first to understand" demonstrates the need to acknowledge another person's or group's point of view, their history, etc. Anything that helps to clarify the pertinent topic at hand before reaching your own biased conclusion. The phrase also demonstrates the power of listening, and moreover, empathy. This is a characteristic that my parents instilled in me from an early age – little did I know that this adage would be so applicable throughout my life. At its core, this simple expression conveys the power of listening and forging empathy between communicators.

Think of someone you know who's a good listener. Ask yourself, *"What is my opinion of this person?"*. Generally, people have high regards and enjoy the company of others who are good listeners. The reason is because without saying a word that person is telling you that they want to understand your point of view.

People enjoy being around good listeners. Why? Because people enjoy talking about themselves. They will associate you with those good feelings they had about themselves when you listened. You'll be viewed as an empathetic and trustworthy person. Learn to understand others first and in turn, they will want to understand you.

Where this applies in our lives is through friendships and relationships. Personal friendships and relationships thrive on the ability for two people to communicate, empathize with the other, and establish commonalities. If you date someone and do not truly listen to them or seek to understand that person, the relationship will not last. The same is true in business. To be a great salesperson, we must learn to keep our mouths shut and our ears open. For some, you may think that to get someone to buy a product, move their investments, or buy insurance you need to convince them to do so. You may start discussing service, investment philosophy and portfolio strategy. You may begin rambling on about benefits you *think* the prospect wants to hear about. You'll practically say ANYTHING because you're waiting for affirmation from the prospect. If this is the case, the deal is already dead. All this does is show the prospect that you are desperate and lack the confidence to really understand them. Don't be frantic. Take your time to truly connect with your prospects.

You must seek first to understand your prospects and clients. If not, how are you able to provide actual benefits and solutions, and know if they are appropriate for that person? Your prospects and clients know this. Otherwise, you're just another salesperson and not a trusted professional.

Seek first to understand your clients and prospects. This is the only way to gain confidence and trust and grow your practice with loyal clients.

CHAPTER 2 - DEVELOPING YOUR PLAN

When it comes to any business, failing to plan is planning to fail. Over time, perspective and focus can change if you do not have an agenda and goals. If you lose focus and perspective, then you most likely will lose your drive. Therefore, you should develop a model week broken down into a daily agenda. This model week is how you will execute to your annual plan. Your annual plan leads directly into your 3- & 5-year plans. I believe that going any farther out than five years is a little misleading. Think of where you were in your life five years ago. How much learning, growing, and changing have you experienced in that time?

Your mission statement will take care of the long-term goals for your practice. There are many questions, both personally and professionally, that you will need to ask yourself to establish your short and long-term plans.

MODEL WEEK

Just like your value statement should convey your purpose to clients and prospects, your daily agenda should provide purpose to every day of the week. On the following page I have outlined a typical model week broken down by day and time. Notice how the model week is only broken down into a few different time brackets. These time brackets will help you stay on task and remain focused on your current activity so that you can be finished with one activity in time to move on to the next.

When I was first introduced to a model week, I'll admit, I was skeptical. My thinking is that I'm a hard worker and can complete tasks as they come along without having to personally hold myself accountable to specific time intervals. WRONG!

After a month, I became frustrated because it felt like I was juggling too many things without truly finishing each project. Accepting defeat, I begrudgingly moved to a model calendar. For a few weeks, I tinkered with my calendar until I was comfortable with each time frame, and guess what happened? I stuck to my schedule, accomplished more in less time, and felt less stressed! Just about every successful advisor in this industry has a model calendar to keep themselves focused and on task.

Your model calendar should consist of blocked sections of time. These sections of time are broken down into the three main areas that will drive your business: Marketing, Meeting with Clients/Prospects, and Casework. Almost all your business-related work should fall into one of these three categories. Once you've established your model calendar, it will dictate your schedule. Neither clients, prospects nor any other outside influence should change your model calendar.

From time to time there may be certain circumstances which require you to deviate from your schedule, and that is okay. My point is that you should be selfish with your goals and the daily tasks necessary to reach them. Once you begin making excuses and letting others take your time from you, it's just a matter of time before you're no longer following your model calendar and begin losing momentum. Consistency is key and the results will speak for themselves.

Once you have established your calendar, you will find that your calendar will start to run your business model and that will force you to complete projects, finish meetings on time, and leave the office at a decent time! There are a couple great ideas that will help make your days easier and your nights more enjoyable by not having to be thinking about the office.

First, before you leave at the end of the day, organize your desk, and write down your list of To-Do's for the next day. When you come in the next morning your office will be fresh, and you will already have your game plan ready for that day! I allot forty-five minutes every morning to review that day's to-do's, meetings, and marketing agenda; afterwards I should have a few minutes leftover to review the morning futures, business reports, or any other articles related to the industry to keep myself fresh and up to date.

Another great idea is to have a spiral bound notebook for taking notes. This spiral bound notebook should be on hand any time you answer the phone, call various departments or companies, etc. The basic purpose of the spiral bound notebook is to serve as one central place where you jot down all your non-meeting notes. Just like most professionals you are busy and if a phone call comes in and you need to write down some information having a notebook handy will prevent you from having to fumble around looking for a sticky note or an extra piece of paper. Also, when you get around to needing that information all you must do is look back in that notebook. This will save you a lot of time and aggravation.

By having a model week and the tools by which to make that week run smoother you should find yourself able to accomplish more each week and to stick to the activities that will bring in new clients and more revenue.

ONE YEAR PLAN

Establishing your one-year plan will help keep your business in focus from month to month. Every year, you should reevaluate your business and establish a new annual plan. This is the only plan that will change from year to year. Let's say that I have established the calendar year for marketing and client service scheduling. So, in December of every year, I will sit down and formulate a plan for next year's business goals to put into action starting January first. To create a well-rounded plan to reach your goals, follow these six steps:

VISION

What is your goal for your business? This should be your mission statement. Reference your mission statement consistently so that you're able to keep in mind why you originally got started in this business. Having a vision is key to achieving success.

GOALS

With your vision as a foundation, what will you accomplish in the upcoming year? Work backwards: start with your annual goals, then systematically break them down into quarterly, monthly, and weekly goals. For example, if your goal is to acquire twenty-four new clients this year, then you'll need to generate at least 2,400 prospects over the next twelve months, which is 200 prospects a month.

PREPARATION

Referencing your business goals, what specific actions must you carry out and what will be your strategy? What will be the costs associated to carry out these activities? How much revenue must be generated to cover these associated costs? Break down your strategy for the year down to quarters, months, and weeks so that you can prepare specific timeframes and strategies.

IMPLEMENTATION

Preparation without implementation is failure. Once you've established your goals and preparation strategies it is important to add specific actions to your model week calendar to make sure that you follow through with those activities. For example, if you hold two seminars a month, be sure to add time to your calendar to follow up with your prospects and hold meetings with them before you move on to your next project. I've found it easier and more focused to concentrate on a particular group of prospects and establish the initial prospect to client conversion process before moving on to the next marketing campaign.

EVALUATION

Review your annual plan monthly. Reflect on your previous month's activities and review the next month's. Do adjustments need to be made? Has the economy changed? Are your marketing strategies still consistent to your target audience?

Your annual plan will incorporate quite a bit of marketing goals, but this should not be your sole focus. It is important to review and plan for client service scheduling, gifting, vacation, budget, implementation of new processes, and other goals and their corresponding activities that will not only help your business grow but make it more efficient and effective. Don't forget to establish personal goals such as paying off a loan, saving money, establishing a college savings plan for your child, going to the gym more often, leaving the office by a specific time every day, and so-on. As with your business plan your personal goals should be broken down into specific monthly and/or weekly actions that can be implemented.

ACCOUNTABILITY

Just as it is important to have a weekly calendar to hold yourself accountable, it's also important to have someone else keep you accountable. Share your plan with your spouse, a co-worker, a manager, a friend, whomever you think appreciates the work you do and expects you to be the best you can be. That person can be there to help motivate you when a time comes where you may be unable or unmotivated to do it on your own.

THREE-YEAR & FIVE-YEAR PLANS

Three and five-year plans are especially important for new advisors or advisors who've changed broker-dealers or agencies. Your plans should include both personal and professional goals. A few questions you may need to ask yourself are:

- What is it about being a financial advisor that motivates me?
- What impact would I like to make on my clients' lives?
- With regards to client service, how do I get the most satisfaction?
- What are my financial goals for myself and how will I accomplish these goals?
- What are the unique ways that I will make my mission statement a reality?
- How much revenue do I need to be producing to achieve my personal and professional goals?
- How many clients and assets under management do I need to have at the end of years three and five to produce that revenue?

Understanding that it may take contacting 100 people to book 10 appointments, to get 5 maybes, and 1 new client, how many people will I need to market to achieve that goal? If I break this down to monthly marketing goals, how many people, starting NOW, do I need to market to every month to ensure I reach my goals?

These are just a few of the questions you should be asking yourself. Your plan should evoke passion and energy, and ultimately re-engage your purpose and enthusiasm for your career.

CHAPTER 3 - BUILDING YOUR NETWORK

Networking can be one of your greatest sources for new prospects. Your network is everyone you know, and have the potential of knowing, and each one of those people is an opportunity for a new client and a referral source to new networks. Networking is an overly broad term and is used to describe any form of communication between a group or individual to foster the sharing of ideas and resources. Your network includes friends, family, co-workers, organizations, groups, professionals, and service providers. Make it a point to establish and reinforce your relationships. These people need to understand what you do for a living and how they can help you. Approaching your network through letters and phone calls gives you the opportunity to continue to build or re-establish those relationships. It also allows you to explain what you do as a financial advisor, acquire your network as clients, and gain access to new networks, organizations, and referrals.

Be prepared to look beyond your network contacts' personal financial needs to examine what types of issues are important for their own personal network. Get in front of your network's coworkers – ask your contact to introduce you to their head of human resources over lunch to meet and discuss presentation opportunities for their employees. Ask your contact if they would invite their co-workers to a lunch for a brief presentation or if they need a guest speaker. Maintain relevance for your network and remember that out of sight is out of mind.

NETWORKING:
COMMUNITY / SOCIAL / PROFESSIONAL ASSOCIATIONS

Some of the most common organizations for local membership by professional men and women include Kiwanis, Rotary, Alumni Associations, and local Chambers of Commerce. These organizations were built by professionals to help promote growth within the community while at the same time organizing to share resources.

There are also formal networking groups created specifically for professionals to share clients and prospects with each other. These can be great opportunities to build your practice by "trading" clients with other local professionals.

Here's an important tip, some of the most productive groups to network within are professional associations, civic groups, and hobby clubs. However, you can network any time or place people congregate – this is your opportunity to really think outside the box and get creative. Networking can happen anytime, anywhere; it doesn't have to be formal. The grocery store, a coffeeshop, or an airline flight are examples of places you can strike up an easy conversation and pivot the conversation.

As with anything in life, it is not just the content of your character that defines you, it is your actions. If you get actively involved with an organization you are passionate about, not only will you reap personal satisfaction, but you will attract prospects who will in turn become clients. However, think carefully before volunteering/running to be a board member or serve on a committee. Often, you will spend more time building the network or group than your business. The key to having healthy participation within your group is to be visible – don't just attend the meetings, volunteer to be a speaker or other visible role.

When attending networking or group meetings, be sure to focus on developing new relationships. Meet at least two or three new people every time. Show a genuine interest in the person and connect with them, don't just collect business cards. Now is your opportunity to use your polished value statement! Introduce yourself to someone who's not engaged in conversation and seek first to understand. Be sure to discuss what your goal is through your networking efforts and let them know that you're creating a network of contacts to build a reciprocating, referral-based business. (Your new contact should eventually be a client, but that needs to be a conversation for another day.)

Look for networking groups that resemble your client base, not your profession. Ask your current client's what organizations they belong to – you may find excellent associations to tap. Imagine that your client is a member of a local human resources association; this is a potential goldmine for your business. Not only can you market to these professionals, but think of the qualified plans, individual employees, and business owners you can be introduced to.

If you are interested in sticking to a networking group specifically, there are a few key things you should keep in mind. First, understand and adapt to the other professionals that are in your group. If you sell life insurance and a life insurance agent is already a member, don't be shy or defeated. Immediately introduce yourself and tell them that you are looking for alliances within the group, not competition. The person will appreciate this candor and will work with you to determine the best course of action to benefit you both. Another way to increase your professional value is in the sharing of ideas. Sometimes this can be just as lucrative as the sharing of prospects. Build knowledge, not just contacts. A successful business-person learns very quickly that the sharing of knowledge is important to growing. Other professionals can share their ideas with you – which methods work, and which don't. This could save you countless hours and hundreds of dollars.

SOCIAL NETWORKING

There are many other networks you can become involved in that hold less competition while being equally rewarding for both prospecting and personally fulfilling. Find a community organization that you are passionate about. A great financial advisor thinks outside the box in many aspects of their personal and professional lives. When it comes to getting involved in your community your first thought should be of things you are passionate about. Do you appreciate nature preservation? Then try looking into a local chapter of the Audubon Society. Do you value history and the preservation of historical sites? Look into local historical / genealogical societies or clubs. Has there been someone close to you that was diagnosed with a specific ailment or disease? Look into local chapters or organizations that help to promote awareness and raise research funds. Some ideas for networking through organizations include being a member of various speaker bureaus, affinity groups, and community organizations such as women's groups and church or non-profit organizations.

NETWORKING WITH CPA'S

Certified Public Accountants are highly respected and trusted by individuals, corporations, and business owners. Even with the advent of do-it-yourself tax preparation software, CPA's are still widely used by individuals and businesses. As such, many people confuse their accountant with someone who can give them investment advice. While there are accountants who're licensed to give financial advice, the networking we will be discussing does not include them. Before prospecting to accountants, it's important to understand that CPA's are the most sought-after network affiliations for financial advisors. They are business professionals just like you and it takes time and patience to be able to forge relationships with them. Forming any professional relationship requires trust and credibility. No CPA is going to refer one of their clients to just any financial advisor that takes them to lunch. They want to make certain that you will treat their client well, offer sound advice, and promote the CPA's value and relationship to the client. Just as it can take months to introduce yourself, establish trust, and convert a prospect into a client, so it will with prospective CPA's.

What can you offer to these professionals? Their first question will most likely be: "What's in it for me?" In this business you must give before you can receive. You must also establish a tangible value along with the professional value you are offering. Sharing revenue is an easy way to establish this. Be sure to check state laws and broker-dealer guidelines. This could be a 50/50 split, or a flat fee based on the number of referrals. Being able to provide additional revenue without the need for more clients could be a great value proposition.

Focusing solely on revenue sharing and ignoring other values you bring will not provide the CPA with a well-rounded relationship; incorporate the entire relationship while conveying value. One way is through client retention. If you and an accountant work with the same client, then you will be able to promote continuity through investments and taxes. By creating an easier environment for a mutual client to handle their finances, both you and the CPA will be able to promote continuity and strengthen that relationship. Just like you, CPA's value the client relationship they have worked hard to establish and maintain. It is extremely important that you convey your commitment to helping him retain more clients.

Another value you can provide is as a professional resource. You should be available to help answer general and specific questions your CPA partner may have regardless of whether it is for a client you will be helping or not. Your professional knowledge can save them countless hours of researching answers to many questions throughout the year. Look for ways to provide tax and legislation updates, economic news, and CPE credits to your CPA network.

When forming a working relationship, it is important to establish a formal alliance as opposed to an informal relationship. A formal alliance is a stronger professional association that will be portrayed and received by a client as a trusted referral. When a client asks their accountant if they know someone who can help them invest their five million dollars, which answer would you rather the CPA give?

"I suggest that you call [your name]. He/She can help you decide what steps to take."

- OR -

"I'm glad you asked. I have a strategic alliance with [your name]. [your name] and I will review your case together to determine the best course of action for you. Would you like me to set up a meeting for the three of us next week?"

The difference in these two scenarios is incentive. In the first scenario, there is no vested interest to recommend you other than you may be a good advisor who has a good personality. The CPA is not personally invested into making sure this client meets you.

In the second scenario, the CPA clearly has a reason to make sure that this client meets with you and will help to set the appointment for you. After you have established your working relationship and coordinated your profit-sharing agreement, then it would be wise to "train" your accounting partner on what to say and set aside certain days and times of the month where you can hold coordinated meetings with the CPA and clients. This creates urgency in the mind of the client and actively involves your CPA in the relationship building process between you and the shared client.

FINDING CPA'S

There are many ways to find CPA's with which to establish a relationship. The easiest is through existing relationships. Start with your own accountant and those of your clients. Also ask friends, family, and networking groups in which you belong. Establishing commonality through a mutual client or friend will give you instant credibility and at the very least ensures a friendly lunch.

Research your state's local CPA society and American Institute of Certified Public Accountants. When researching firms to contact, make certain they do not already offer brokerage or investment services. It's easy to get caught up in the details of researching your prospects and lose sight of the objective, which is to speak with CPA's. Don't be afraid to pick up the phone and start talking, the same principles apply to CPA prospects that apply to prospective clients: numbers and consistency. Consistently calling 10 accounting firms a week will yield more results and have you sitting down face-to-face with at least one qualified CPA a week. Be selective about how many CPA's you'll be working with. This is a long-term business partnership that can benefit both of you tremendously and over time you may find that you have one or two excellent partners that help meet your needs.

TELEPHONE CALL TO A CPA

Hello, this is [your name] with [practice name]. May I speak with [CPA's name], please?

[CPA's name], this is [your name] with [practice name] here in [location]. A mutual client of ours, [name of client], suggested that I contact you. Do you have a moment to speak?

[Name of client] mentioned that you had done some good work for them this past year in preparing their tax return. [Name of prospect] said that you were thorough, timely, and reasonably priced, and highly recommended your service. Do you remember working on their case?

The reason for my call is that I have strategic alliances with a few other CPA's in the area and I'm looking to develop a new relationship with a CPA who is committed to providing the same high-quality work that I do. I'd like to meet you for lunch or coffee where we could learn about each other's business and discuss the type of relationship that can mutually benefit our clients.

INTERVIEW WITH CPA

[CPA's name], I am continuously developing relationships with local professionals whose services could benefit my clients. After hearing the high regards [name of referring clients] has of you, I already feel comfortable discussing how we can benefit

each other's practices. I'd like to learn more about how you run
your practice and the types of services you offer your clients;
then explain to you the types of services that I provide for my
clients. If it makes sense, we could then discuss developing a
relationship that would be mutually beneficial to our clients.
How does that sound?
Great.
Tell me a little about the type of tax work that you do.
Do you specialize in any a particular area?
What type of client is best suited for the services you provide?
Are you accepting new clients?
How do you typically acquire new clients?
What are your fee structures?
Ok, let me take a moment to explain the types of services I
provide my clients as a
financial advisor.

From the CPA's perspective, there is much to gain from a formal strategic alliance. Revenue sharing, increased client retention, and professional resources can be a tremendous value to any practice. It is up to you to prove that you can deliver on your promises.

In closing, the same approach you take with CPA's can also be applied to other professionals such as attorneys, real estate agents, recruiting agencies, sports agents, and physicians. These alliances must be nurtured and may take time to cultivate. Once established, these professional relationships can be an integral part of your business model.

CHAPTER 4 – MARKETING

Marketing is not just something you do if you want to be successful in this business. Marketing is who you are. When coming up with your weekly calendar there should be no time allocated for just "marketing." That time should be allotted for specific marketing activities, and if you want to be a successful financial advisor, you must always be marketing. Family functions, parties, golf outings, the doctor's office, etc. Wherever you can meet people there is the opportunity to market.

Marketing is defined as an integrated communications-based process through which individuals and communities discover that existing and newly-identified needs and wants may be satisfied by the products and services of others." There's one word that stands out to me immediately - communications. Take a moment and think of how many people you come across every day. Seriously.

Try to guess how many people you have or could say hello to on an average day. People you pass on your way into the office, people at the grocery store, in line for lunch, at the gas station, at your church, etc. Now think of how many people you pass on your daily commute! My point being is that there are a lot of people that you interact with every single day!

Marketing consists primarily of numbers, consistency, and saturation. The more people you can introduce yourself to, the more opportunities you will have to communicate your services. As discussed previously, it's important to learn how to deal with rejection as quickly as possible. The easiest way to understand rejection is to know that people don't reject other people, they reject the timing.

Imagine walking into a department store because you need to buy a new pair of pants. A sales associate walks up to you and says, *"Good morning. Is there anything I can help you with today?"* What is your response? Seriously, what have you said in the past? Well, I know what my response has been almost 100% of the time: *"No, I'm good"* or *"I'm just looking around."*

I know the associate was only doing their job and offering great customer service, but I had my own priorities and "confidence" in what I wanted. However, 10 minutes later I'm trying to find that associate because I need their help! I was not rejecting that person; I was simply rejecting the timing.

One of the best pieces of business advice I've ever received is this:

PEOPLE DON'T REJECT OTHER PEOPLE, THEY JUST REJECT THE TIMING

Marketing is also about consistency and saturation. Conduct a seminar the same way, every time. Your delivery will be strong and direct. Not only will you be viewed as a professional in your field, but you will portray yourself as a professional speaker as well. If you advertise in a newspaper don't just put your ad in for one month, you should schedule the ad to run for at least six months. It is important for your target audience to see your name, face, and practice on a consistent basis. This creates and builds credibility and promotes you as an expert in your field.

An overriding factor for investors to consider when working with a financial advisor is their perception of that advisor's expertise. It is paramount that you position yourself as an expert in your field who can help your clients solve problems and create solutions. You must continue to reinforce that view, and this is where saturation comes in to play. Don't just have one newspaper or magazine that you advertise with, submit your expertise to multiple media sources. Get interviewed with a local television or radio program, newspaper, or magazine. Your goal should be top of mind, through your marketing efforts, to members of your niche market.

Consistency is also important when it comes to the day to day running of your practice. Make sure that you keep your unspoken commitments to your clients. For instance, if you send a birthday card to a client, they will expect another card the next year and so on. If you have a client that becomes ill and you send a get-well card – that is very nice, but what if a friend of theirs is also a client and they become sick six months later and you don't send them a card? It is likely that neither will know whether the other received a card from you, but there is a chance that they may. This barely touches on the extreme need for systems in your practice, so commit to reviewing your outreach practices on a consistent basis.

Another good rule of thumb is that it is easier to keep a client by providing top-notch service than having to replace clients who are enticed by other advisors to leave your practice. Client retention is equally as important as converting prospects into new clients.

Aside from networking, there are three core ways to obtain new clients:

- Advertising
- Seminars
- Referrals

One must first narrow down the audience you will be targeting for your services. In doing so you will create a niche market where you can be known as the go-to expert.

FIND YOUR NICHE

When it comes to marketing there are so many ways to attract new prospects and clients. You could spend all your time bouncing from idea to idea with no real results and before you know it, you're flat on your back and out of the business. This book provides plenty of practical ideas and specific examples on how to market, but you will need to decide which ideas you will apply to your practice. It doesn't matter how much you market your services, if you can't get prospects on the phone and in the door then all your work was wasted. In any business, marketing is all about numbers and consistency and it is particularly important to know that marketing does not always yield immediate results. That is why it is important to always be marketing! Often you won't see results from your efforts today until months down the road.

Define your marketing strategy into five parts:

- Who will you be targeting?
- Why are you targeting these specific people?
- What are the specific services you'll be offering this group?
- When will you be contacting this target prospect source?
- How will you market to these prospects?

Once you've answered these questions you will have found your niche market and your means for reaching and engaging potential prospects. The next steps will be to learn more about your target audience and then properly leverage your skill set through marketing.

Now that you have your niche market, it is time to learn about your audience. Let's say that you are going to pursue orthopedic surgeons. Your first step will be to learn as much as you can about this area of expertise. It will be important for you to having a basic understanding of joint and ligament structure and stay up to date on some of the cutting-edge research being done in the field. Subscribe to the most popular or widely read trade magazines so that you can stay continually up to date on the industry. Stay informed on local events and trade shows where you can attend or host a booth.

Establishing contacts in any industry is as easy as quick phone call to introduce yourself and a compliment about their excellent publication or seminar. Your niche market should be an area that intrigues you – reactions, knowledge, and discussions should be genuine on your part. Advertise according to your audience and recognize that professionals respect other professionals who set themselves apart from the competition and provide tailored services. You can be the well-rounded advisor that your niche prospects are looking for by engaging yourself enthusiastically within that field.

ADVERTISING

Just like any other aspect of marketing, advertising, if done properly can yield good results. Many financial advisors advertise products or services, thinking that this will engage prospects and cause them to act. This thinking is completely wrong. Would you decide to go to a restaurant because they put their menu in the newspaper? Probably not.

Advertising is a way to establish an emotional bond with your audience and tell them that you understand their financial/emotional needs. It is also important to understand the power of reinforcement. One advertisement by itself will probably not prompt many people to act, but if you have the same ad on the same page of the same newspaper every week for a month, then you will be reaching the same people and reinforcing their need to take action. In the case of a direct mail, it is more effective to send the same mailer to the same 1,000 people once a month for five months than to send one mailer to 1,000 people, once. This applies to any advertising whether it is on the internet, in a magazine, a television commercial, etc.

When executed properly, advertising should be engaging and captivating for your audience. Your target audience needs to feel emotionally compelled to reach out and act, not logically compelled. A few examples of emotionally engaging headlines are:

How much money did your Insurance Company give back to you last month?
Who do you think pays for all those big budget commercials?
I'm Sorry Son, We Can't Afford for You to Go to College.
Why Your Neighbors Vacation in Hawaii, While You Take "Extended Weekends."
C'mon, You Know There is A Better Way to Real Wealth
You Just Don't Know the Right Questions to Ask

These headlines grab your attention and draw you in emotionally. Next, let's compare them to the following "logical" headlines:

Call Now for a Quote on Your Insurance!
Are You on Track for Retirement?
Learn How Mutual Funds Can Help You Find Real Wealth!

These headlines don't evoke the same emotional response, yet these are the headlines that flood our newspapers, magazines, billboards, and televisions every day. I can tell you that the people reaping the real rewards from these advertisements are those who are selling the advertising space!

PRINT/TELEVISION/RADIO/
INTERNET ADVERTISING

One should approach advertising with the understanding that the audience must be targeted appropriately and have a message that speaks directly to them: Captivating Headline, Motivating Substance, and an Immediate Benefit. Knowing your audience is important when deciding on your message. Do you think that you will get many responses if you advertise renter's insurance in a Home & Gardens magazine? What if you advertise retirement income solutions in a parenting magazine? Ultimately, the goal of any advertising is to establish commonality and break the initial barrier between you and your audience, which is, *"I don't know you and I don't trust you."*

This is the most significant hurdle for prospects to overcome and if you can introduce yourself and your services before a prospect meets you, the conversation will be that much easier. Advertisements, especially through TV and radio, are a way for you to say to your audience "I understand your concerns. Others have felt the same way. I have the solution you are looking for."

Television and online advertising are powerful mediums for promoting your practice, but the perception is that only large corporations or practices with deep budgeting pockets can afford this. This is not necessarily true; most of your costs will be in producing your commercial and the medium you're advertising through. These costs can be significantly reduced using modern technology, i.e.

smart phone, and social media. When considering television and internet advertising it is important to consider
cost vs. effectiveness vs. time. Generally, a fifteen second
advertisement is so short that it is difficult to effectively
convey your message to your audience. A sixty second
advertisement does not have to have a rushed format, and
therefore can better connect with your audience and leave
a longer lasting impression. Of course, a sixty second
commercial will cost more to run, but could be well worth
the extra investment for the impact you can have with
your target audience.

A narrated commercial will probably be the most cost
and marketing effective if done properly. The presentation can be a narrative over still shots of canned financial
photos with a photo of you at the end with your contact
information. A great idea is to see if you can get a local
radio personality or local "celebrity" to do the voice-over.
Surprisingly, this can be very inexpensive.

As with direct mailers, your engagement message
should be emotionally engaging and reinforced both
verbally by the announcer and visually by putting those
exact words on the screen. When choosing the right vi-
suals for your commercial, it is important to engage with
your appropriate target audience, keeping your scenes
engaging, clean and crisp. A slow zooming close-up of an
egg in a bird's nest can be much easier on your audience's
eyes than a broad pan of traders on the NYSE trading
floor. Reinforce your narration through words on the
screen throughout your commercial. This can be done

by having the words appear verbatim as they are spoken, the phrases appear all at once during the narration, or impact words and phrases from the narration appear on the screen. Both the verbal and written message should present your points using nouns and verbs. Try to leave out as many words that are not impact words to keep your idea on point. Whether you provide the narration, or you hire someone, be sure to keep a conversational tone; many times, your audience will lose trust if the narration is too comical or sounds like a sales pitch.

Once you have your commercial consumer-ready get a digital copy to e-mail to prospects, clients, family, and friends. Have them distribute this commercial to their network and so-on. Post the commercial on social media sites. It is important to reach as many people as possible to emotionally engage and introduce yourself as the solution.

Depending on your budget, it may be possible to extend your commercial into an infomercial which can further engage your audience, explain your services, and create familiarity with your practice. An infomercial can be a good way to promote your knowledge, expertise, and evoke an even stronger emotional bond between you and your prospects. The key to an effective infomercial is that you should only emphasize one main concern your audience is facing. This should be your expertise and focus on your niche market's concern. If you try to sell more than one idea it becomes unfocused and therefore people will lose interest. Once you have established this main concern it is imperative to come up with as many selling points as possible to prove your expertise and reinforce your solutions. For instance, if you're focusing on retirement income for retirees, then you should promote numerous features and benefits of your practice's retiree income solutions and list them in order of importance. Examples:

Feature:	Monthly check from investments
Benefit:	Guaranteed ability to pay all your bills
Feature:	Name specific beneficiaries
Benefit:	Control your legacy from the grave
Feature:	Longevity and income analysis
Benefit:	Maintain control and flexibility of your assets

If you are considering incorporating a testimonial from a client there are a few things to consider. First, be aware of FINRA, SEC, and your firm's rules and regulations. This is a closely monitored area of advertising and you should know exactly what is permissible. If you use client testimonials, be certain that it is not scripted. This person needs to be able to relate to your audience as much as you do and maintain believability.

Radio and podcasts are other great mediums for targeting your specific niche market for a relatively low cost. Most radio stations have their demographics as well analyzed as TV and will be able to provide you with those specific demographics and times specific to the market you are targeting. The key is to be engaging enough for a consumer's attention to be primarily focused on your sales point. These listeners are not solely captivated by the medium and are usually engaged in another activity such as driving, working, or exercising. Making your ad engaging does not mean adding a catchy jingle or special effects sounds – these gimmicks can take away (but not always) from your ad. It is important to have your message speak for itself. Less is more. After much research and trial and error, I've found a great way to make your radio advertisement believable and engaging is to have a local radio host narrate your commercial or have the commercial recited live by that radio personality. The local radio host is someone the target audience already knows and trusts which makes your advertisement even more believable.

Radio ads are sometimes used for reinforcement of other advertisements through TV or print and help to continue promoting you as an expert in your field. Because of this, it is important to convey the same message and evoke the same emotional response that you are conveying in other advertising mediums. Continuity is Key.

Finally, advertising is useless if the audience does not act upon your message. It is necessary for you to decide what your call to action will be for your radio and TV advertisements. The Ads themselves will not create new clients, and it is up to you to decide how you want to engage the audience and what their next step should be.

- Do you want them to pick up the phone to call your office and schedule an appointment?
- Do you want to drive people to your website to fill out a complimentary risk evaluation form?
- Do you want people to e-mail you for their free copy of a "how-to-invest" workbook?
- Know your content and tailor your advertisement so that your audience will be engaged to act.

GET INTERVIEWED

Imagine for a moment that you're a surgeon who's in need of investment advice. First, the abundance of television, radio, print, and internet advertisements have created a blur of resources available to you. Next, your coworkers and colleagues either have different advisors who are all highly recommended or are like you and at somewhat of a loss as to where to get the best advice. Also thrown in your attorney, accountant, friends, and family who all have different recommendations and opinions.

Pretty frustrating isn't it? As a financial advisor it is important to set yourself apart from the competition by speaking directly to your prospective audience. Establish yourself as a trusted expert who can help those surgeons (seniors, engineers, target market...) understand complex financial issues that face them directly. One of the most effective ways to do this is through interviews with local and/or targeted media.

Before deciding on what to talk about, who to contact, or any other aspect of a media interview it is important to determine your strengths and weaknesses when it comes to communication. If you are a fantastic writer and can convey complex ideas into simple, easy to understand concepts through written words, then writing a guest article for a publication may be the best way to utilize your strengths. Conversely, if you are camera shy or use the words "like" and "umm" a lot, then you probably would not do well on a television interview.

After deciding your preferred method of media communications, contact local and targeted media outlets to let them know you are a financial expert that would be willing to offer yourself as a resource for their medium. Research the different media outlets and narrow down media contacts within those industries. Next, continuously promote yourself as an added value to the target media. This must be a win-win situation where you benefit from exposure and the media outlet benefits from added value and free financial expertise for their audience.

Once you have been interviewed be sure to send the article or link to video to all your clients and prospects. With permission you may be able to distribute the interview to other media outlets for redistribution. Through regular media exposure as an industry expert you will raise your credibility throughout your target audience, current clients, and prospects.

MAGAZINE ARTICLES

Another form of free advertising is by becoming a contributing writer to a magazine, newspaper, or other periodical. As with your approach to being interviewed by a media outlet, being a contributing writer can give you instant credibility. A letter, phone call, or e-mail to begin the conversation will be up to you. Here is a sample letter to the editor:

Hello, my name is [your name] and I am a local financial advisor here in [city]. I thoroughly enjoy [name of periodical]. The articles are informative, and I frequently reference your publication to find [niche].

The reason for my letter is to offer myself as a resource for you. I would like to discuss submitting articles as a contributing writer. I currently publish a monthly newsletter which covers real-time issues on topics such as the housing market, retirement planning, and interest rates. Because of the lack of financial understanding by the public, I believe this would be a great opportunity to provide added value to your readers.

I am confident your audience will find my articles engaging, informative, and what they expect from your publication.

Thank you for your consideration – I will call you next week to set up a time for us to discuss this in more detail.

If you decide to begin the conversation through a letter, it is imperative that you follow up with a phone call. The point of the letter and the phone call is not to get a yes or a no to being published, but a fifteen to twenty-minute interview to discuss your contributions in more detail. Get in front of the person making the decisions for the magazine or newspaper so that they can meet you in person and you can sell them on the benefits that your writings will have for their publication.

Some publications will consider this as advertising and therefore you will be subject to the costs associated with advertisements. However, others will have contracts in which you receive compensation for your articles or will ask you to submit monthly and will publish on an "as needed" basis. Therefore, it is important to meet the publisher or editor to discuss these details and work out a win-win deal for you both.

E-MAIL

Marketing effectively through e-mail can be tough to accomplish. There are CAN-SPAM laws that prohibit unwanted mass e-mails, and even without these laws, you don't want to be perceived as some fly-by-night financial advisor. I believe that the most ethical and appropriate way to market through e-mail is by building your own e-mail list through contacts, clients, and prospects. A monthly newsletter is a great e-mail marketing technique that provides value, your contact information, and a non-intimidating way for contacts to learn more about you and your practice.

It's important to not saturate your clients and prospects with too many e-mails. You might love what you do for a living, but most of your clients hired you because they don't. Keep clients and prospects abreast of important information regarding your practice and opportunities that are available, but if you send too many e-mails, then more than likely your future e-mails will be ignored and considered a waste of time.

WEBSITE

A website should be a huge priority. Everyday millions of people are searching for information. Your web site should reflect who you are, what areas you specialize in and your contact information. Most people are more likely to log-on to the internet to review your business than they are to call your office. When advertising through other mediums such as print or television it is essential that your web address stands out and is equally as visible as all your other contact information. Many broker dealers provide template web addresses for their advisors which will provide some basic information, a photo, and an opportunity for someone to contact you. If you are an independent advisor there may be more freedom and flexibility in how you run your website and the content you're able to provide.

CHAPTER 4 – MARKETING

Personally, I enjoy websites which are simple, offer basic information on the advisor (much like a biography), and include a suitability questionnaire. A suitability questionnaire is a simple marketing technique that will help the advisor find prospective clients that fit their ideal client profile and give the prospect the feeling of anonymity while filling out the simple Q&A. The questionnaire should ask a few questions, such as age range, income level, investable assets, areas of importance and contact information. Overall, it should take a person less than one minute to submit and then, voila, you have a warm prospect. One of the reasons people like the internet is because it is impersonal and non-confrontational. If you want to buy something or know the services a company offers there is no salesman there to make you feel pressured. An easy-to-use, non-intimidating website that offers answers to the questions your prospects may have can promote a positive impression of you and your practice.

A website that no one can find is a waste of your time and money. That is why it is equally as important to generate web traffic to your website. This requires work and ongoing effort to promote your website. The goal is to get as many people as possible to visit your website. The reason is two-fold: First, marketing is about consistency and numbers. The more people you have coming to your website the greater the chance someone will request a consultation or at minimum, literature. Second, build your site popularity on current search engines. The more people that click through to your site, the more popular it becomes and the higher your website's search engine ranking. The higher your search engine ranking the more relevance your site.

When you need to look up information on the internet and you enter key words into a search engine, how often do you go to the second, third, sixth, seventieth page of relevant links to find an answer? If you're like me, it is rare to go to the third page of search engine results. Therefore, it is important to get your information to the top of the search engine results list – because if you aren't, then no one will find you.

Search engines use complex algorithms to determine the results from a search in their information retrieval system and there are certain characteristics your website should possess to get optimal page ranking. These include relevant term frequency, proximity, the location of those relevant terms on your webpage, link analysis (basically, your site's relevance to the times), website popularity, date of last publication or update, etc. There are numerous ways in which to do this and all of them will help. When it comes to website popularity and traffic, it is essential to know that the sum of the parts is most important.

First, contact everyone you know and see if they have a web page, blog, or site where they may do business (as long as the site's content does not reflect poorly on you) and see if you can put a banner advertisement on their webpage where people can click and go to your webpage. This may or may not generate new clients for you, but remember, your goal is to get as much traffic to your website as possible and contacting friends and family should be the quickest and easiest way to get started.

SEMINARS

Seminars are an extremely focused way of attracting the type of prospect you want for your practice, establishing credibility, and earning trust. The most important ways to host a successful seminar are:

1. INVITE A TARGETED AUDIENCE

You may only have a handful of attendees if you do not narrow down your seminar topic and focus on a specific group of people. For instance – if you are focusing on young parents, you will have a better response sending your invitation to local daycares a call on a mother's group to request a speaking opportunity, chances are good that if you tell them you would like to speak on qualified retirement plan distributions they will politely decline your offer. However, if you promote your timely College Planning seminar, they will make room for you to speak ASAP.

2. CREATE THE RIGHT INVITATION

This is usually the most misunderstood part of a financial advisor's seminar pipeline. Your invitation should be created to attract specific demographics of people for the specific seminar you are hosting. The title of your seminar should be emotionally engaging and the same principles that were discussed in creating direct mailings should apply to your seminar invitations, with only a couple subtle differences. Your bullet points following the headline should sell your audience on why they need to attend your seminar. As with the bullet points within a direct mailing piece, they should be compelling and offer potential solutions to a broad group of people within your target audience.

3. LOCATION, LOCATION, LOCATION

What works for you does not necessarily work for your audience. It may be ok to hold a client event or seminar at your office, but not a prospect seminar. The location for your seminar should be a neutral environment. The atmosphere should also be targeted toward the audience that will be attending. An established restaurant that appeals to both upper- and middle-class clientele is ideal for hosting a relaxed seminar. Some attendees will assume that if you are hosting a seminar at a restaurant that you will also be providing food. I've never fed prospects a meal at a seminar, but rather provided snacks and drinks. I have never had a bad experience with this and do not think that not feeding my prospects has cancelled a deal. Besides, you don't want "plate-lickers" to show up to your seminar just for the food. If you have targeted specific groups of people (trade groups, professional organizations), then it would be best to host your seminar at their facility or at a place of their choosing. This helps to ensure maximum attendance with respects to location of the seminar.

4. YOU ARE YOUR SEMINAR

The purpose of any marketing activity is to generate business. When it comes to seminars, the best value is to present the material yourself. You invited these prospects for the sole purpose of converting them to clients. Position yourself as the expert and sell yourself!

If you invite a wholesaler to come present to your audience, they will view him or her and the company they represent as the professional, not you. You are simply the middleman who put together, paid for, and hosted an event. Instead, welcome everyone personally who attends and when it comes time to present the topic, stand up, prove your expertise, and earn their trust.

5. BOOK APPOINTMENTS AT THE SEMINAR

This is a critical mistake I've witnessed many advisors commit, including myself! When I first began hosting seminars it took me a few presentations to learn this valuable lesson. I would get my prospects engaged, informed, and concerned, then ask my prospects to fill out the evaluation form so that I could follow up later this week. To my utter amazement, I booked less than ten percent of the attendees for appointments! The hurdle you must get over is that you will convey yourself as someone who hosted the seminar to inform people that you can help them in the areas discussed and would like to meet with them.

Ha! Might as well not even host the seminar, huh? You must be unique in every area of your marketing expertise. Figure out a way to make sure that everyone personally brings you their evaluation form. This is the time that you have your calendar in plain sight and you look over their evaluation form and ask them what time that week would be best to meet to discuss their questions.

Be assumptive – these people attended your seminar for a reason. The logical conclusion at the end of the seminar is that they will either want to meet with you because they need your help, or they won't. Waiting a day or two will only change people's minds from wanting to sit down with you to deciding that the topic was not that important, or they can wait. Know your responses to objections and when someone gives you an objection, confront them, politely. If someone says they would like to wait and speak with their spouse, tell them that the spouse was not here to hear this information and therefore won't know the true importance of setting an appointment. Tell them that you will go ahead and set a meeting and just have them bring their spouse along – personalize it and tell them that you would do the same thing with your own spouse. The main point being – set the appointment!

SEMINAR DO'S AND DON'TS

- Never send detailed info on your topic in advance – if people already have the info, why do they need to listen to your presentation? An informative two to four sentence synopses of the topic should be sufficient.

- Always know your topic. The group/organization wants a knowledgeable professional who can answer questions and is confident. A rule of thumb is three hours of practice/study for every one hour of presentation. Always memorize the presentation but have an outline that you refer to. Your audience will appreciate the fact that you want to remain on topic. Also, I haven't found having a PowerPoint adds enough value to a presentation to say that you need one every time – this is up to your discretion and the topic being presented.

- Always be truthful. If an audience member asks you a question you don't know – do not guess. If you don't know the answer tell them that is a great question and that you would be happy to get back in touch with them the next day with the answer. Not only do you convey honesty, but this is a great way to follow up with this prospect to set a meeting!

- Always have handouts on your topic. I've found the best combination to be a pocket folder containing generalized details on your presentation topic - you don't want them to have all the information at their fingertips, just enough to make sure they need your help, your bio with a list of services, and a magnetic business card.

If you hand out a ton of information the whole packet will be thrown away – remember, people are busy and don't have the time to read through a whole bunch of information – that's another reason why they need your help.

- Always have a seminar evaluation form! Before you begin your seminar ask everyone to take out the form. Tell them that this is your report card on your presentation and at the end you would like everyone's honest opinion of how well received the presentation was.

- Always have extra pens. Be prepared!

- Always get your audience involved – ask them questions and get them to ask questions. Remember back to when you were in school. The teacher would ask if anyone had any questions and no one would raise their hand or ask any questions. All it would take is one person to speak up and then suddenly everyone has questions and comments. You want your audience to think and participate, not just absorb, you want them to think about their own circumstance and talk about it – this will help raise their level of personal concern.

- Recognize opportunities - some seminars are best to leave questions till the end, others while you are presenting. Either way, your goal is not to answer every question but to be able to lead and encourage these attendees to book an appointment with you:

"These are all fantastic questions and I can tell that this is a topic that is especially important to each of you. Each person's situation is unique and a certain strategy for one person may be totally wrong for another. Here's what I can do, I'm leaving in a few minutes for another appointment – I would ask that each of you take this time to fill out the evaluation form. When you bring me your evaluation form, we can set up a time for you and your spouse to sit down with me in the next week or two. I offer a complimentary consultation where your questions can be answered, and we can determine the strategy that works best for you."

- Always follow up with your attendees to book an appointment. Be sure to ask if they would like to be added to your monthly newsletter.
- Always mail a handwritten note to the group's contact thanking them for opportunity to speak to their group.

INEXPENSIVE SEMINARS

Research your city and the surrounding areas to find community organizations. Most organizations have monthly or quarterly meetings and are always in need for volunteer speakers.

Examples include newcomer's clubs, auto clubs, mother's clubs, CPA societies, legal societies, etc... The key to ensuring that you will be given the opportunity to speak for these organizations is to match your target audience with specific and relevant topics.

SEMINAR REQUEST SCRIPT

A typical conversation regarding a college savings seminar may go like this:

Hello, my name is [your name]. I'm a local financial advisor here in [city]. It's a passion and priority of mine to help other people make sense of the various strategies in saving for college by passing along the importance of financial education through my clients, hosting seminars, or being involved in community outreach programs (or list an organization you are involved in). The reason for my call is to offer myself as a speaker for your group.

...

I completely understand your hesitation − in fact, I hear that often. I just introduced myself and you don't know me or my credentials. First, let me say that I know firsthand the importance of parents making the right college saving decisions early so that they have options later - however, I have found that many parents start too late, don't under- stand all the different strategies available to them or do not know the correct way to save given their own unique circumstance. Would you agree?

I'll dispel some of the myths and answer plenty of questions – the seminar is very informal. There is no fee for me to come speak to your group – it's a great way for me to get out into the community and meet folks. Most organizations request that I speak on _____. Would that be the best topic for your group?

...

Great. How often are your meetings?

...

My schedule is full this month, however, my calendar is open next month. What time are your meetings held?

...

Perfect. Along with the actual seminar I will also provide everyone with a handout that lists everything I talk about. I've found that to be popular. How many members do you expect at the meeting?

This script can be tailored to any seminar topic. Just like any other marketing endeavor, you will probably receive at least one "no" during your conversation. It's important to acknowledge their reason for saying no but continue with the script.

Another consideration is that if the group likes your presentation you should have a list of other seminars you offer on hand. Tell the president of the group that they can keep this list and call on you if they would like you to come back and present another topic. Also, ask the person with whom you scheduled the seminar if they have a newsletter and if they could add your contact information or whether you could submit articles to their newsletter. Be sure to ask this after you've given your presentation, not before.

CLIENT REFERRALS

Many clients know people who could use your services, but it is up to you to help your client understand the different areas where you can help. Think of it this way, one client group may have rolled over a large sum of money from a previous employer that you have been managing for about a year. Their understanding of your areas of focus center around their accounts, so when a friend strikes up a conversation with them and says they need to set up a custodial account for their granddaughter, you are not even thought of – or, your name is mentioned offhanded as a possible resource.

This type of scenario happens all too often, and that is because you have not communicated to your current clients how important they are. It is one thing to do a great job for your clients and have them feel good about being your clients, and another thing altogether to have an army of ambassadors out promoting your services to people they know about your practice.

The first step to building your practice through referrals is to always give great advice and service. Clients will want to help you grow because they believe in the work you do for them. At the end of every client meeting the conversation should turn to their working relationship with you and ask them for feedback regarding your services. Be honest with your clients and tell them you would like to have a practice built entirely on referrals.

Example:

"[client name], you've told me how much you appreciate our open communication and that the work we've done together has made you feel more secure with your retirement plans. Personally, I love working with you and would like to meet more people like you. It's a goal of mine to build a practice based on referrals from clients so that I'm able to spend more time focusing on you and your needs and less time away from the office marketing.
Would you do me a favor and take the next few minutes brainstorming with me on some people you know that you'd feel comfortable making a casual introduction?"

It's important to get your clients discussing names and ideas. To be effective, have a list of life events, hobbies, and club memberships that will help guide the brainstorming activity. Show your list of thought starters to your clients and just let them talk. Write down names and information, continuously saying, *"Tell me more about [prospect]."*

After you've learned about all the people your clients discussed with your conversation should be as follows:

"[client], do you remember when we first started working together? Do you remember your skepticism and the building of trust between us that took time to develop? Do you have any regrets about your decision for us to work together?

Well, I would like for you to convey that personal story of how we developed our professional relationship to your friend, [prospect], and let them know how I have helped you since then."

Sometimes it will be necessary to respond to some push back from your client. If so, I've found the following script to be highly effective:

"If they try to explain away that they don't need a financial advisor or that they already have one, just remember you had a similar reaction when we first spoke. Ask if they would at least talk to me, keep an open mind, and maybe I can answer some questions they might have or at the very least give them some suggestions. I will call them [day of the week] to introduce myself. As always, my conversations are kept confidential. Does this sound fair to you?"

People feel good when they are needed. By sticking to the script you should also have them asking the question, "Why should I keep my financial advisor a secret?" Also, don't expect your clients to know the financial situation of their friends and family. If they get too focused on this explain that confidentiality is paramount to your practice and you're just looking for introductions.

Set aside one afternoon a week just for calling back referrals. Make it the same day and time every week so that you can give your clients firm dates as to when you'll be calling these referrals. This is important because by setting a deadline, the client will feel more obligated to contact the referral as soon as possible.

FROM REFERRAL TO CLIENT

When it comes to contacting the referral, the goal of this conversation should be to build rapport and then dive right into the prospect script. You already have credibility through your mutual friend, so these conversations tend to be very casual at first. If you are not careful, the conversation will remain casual because the referral does not want to insult you and thinks they are doing their friend a favor by speaking with you for a few minutes. It is imperative that you treat the referral as you would any other prospect. The following is the general conversation introduction you should have with a referral:

Hello, may I speak with [referral's name]?
Hi, [referral's name]. This is [your name] with [name of your practice] here in [local city name]. I was asked to give you a call because your name came up in a conversation that I was having with a mutual friend [client's name]. Did [client's name] mention that I would be calling you?
Great! (Referring Client) mentioned that you (love to cook/ like to garden, etc.) I'm glad that (client's name) mentioned I'd

be calling you. I'm curious, what did (he/she) say about how we've been working together?

At this point, the conversation should go directly into the prospect script which is discussed more in Chapter Five under the Setting the Appointment section.

If you are calling a referral to invite them to a dinner, event, or seminar then it is important to not press them on any financial issues – the conversation should be as follows:

Hello, may I speak with [referral's name]?

Hi, [referral's name]. This is [your name] with [name of your practice] here in [local city name]. I was asked to give you a call because your name came up in a conversation that I was having with a mutual friend [client's name]. Did [client's name] mention that I would be calling you?

[WAIT FOR RESPONSE]

Great! By the way, (referrer) mentioned that you (have a taste for luxury cars/love to golf/ like to garden, etc.)

[WAIT FOR RESPONSE]

I mentioned to [client's name] that I am hosting a [name of event] and asked him if he knew anyone that would be interested in attending. The event is scheduled for [date and time] and we have a spot open for you.

Describe the event and establish more rapport. This phone call is important because it gets the formalities out of the way so that while you are at the event with the referral and the client no one feels pressured.

TOP 50 MARKETING STRATEGIES

Marketing not only includes ways to get new clients, but ways to keep existing clients. It should be your goal to maintain 100% client retention. Never give your client a reason to leave your practice. It's easier to grow your business when your prospects are not having to replace clients and assets that have left your practice.

The following are my Top 50 Marketing Strategies. These include ideas on prospecting, as well as client retention. The ideas set forth here can be used for both prospects and clients. Make certain that you add your own individualism to any idea you incorporate – it helps add personality and character to the endeavors that you incorporate into your practice.

When it comes to events, it is up to you how many people you invite, how you target your audience or attendees, and whether it is a client bring a friend event or strictly for prospects. When hosting an event always bring your camera! Take candid photos as well as coordinated group and individual photos. When taking individual photos or those of husbands and wives always take one of the two together and another of them with you. People love looking at photos of themselves and it helps to create memories. When hosting a client bring-a-friend event where your clients bring guests, make it abundantly clear that you need their help and that the reason you are holding this event, whether it is intimate or a large group, is to show appreciation to your current clients and get new clients. Let your clients know up front how important they are in helping you grow your practice – trust me, they will understand, and at times be your greatest marketing asset.

1. MAGNETIC BUSINESS CARDS

It's quite easy to misplace (polite for throw-away) another person's business card. However, most anyone will slap a magnet on their refrigerator or cabinet without thinking twice, regardless of what the magnet says. I make a joke of it when I give out my business card. I give my client/prospect a business card saying here is the card you will lose, and here (as I'm handing them the magnetic card) is the card you won't lose. It creates a memorable moment linking you to the good feeling they had when you said it.

2. BIRTHDAY CARDS

This is a quite simple but powerful marketing tool. The key here is consistency. Once you begin mailing birthday cards, it is imperative that you don't forget to send them every year thereafter. People mostly remember not receiving a card if you've established a pattern and then break it. Some advisors even send birthday cards to prospects as well – that is up to your own personal discretion.

3. HOLIDAY CARDS

Again, another form of marketing/client retention. I mail two holiday cards every year to all my clients, prospects, and network: 4th of July and Christmas. The 4th of July card is a reminder of our patriotic ties as Americans. The Christmas card is a simple photo card with a holiday picture of my family and a simple holiday greeting. It is the same Christmas card I send to family and friends.

4. GIFTS

Before giving a gift to someone be sure to review the regulatory compliance guidelines and your broker-dealer. Giving gifts is a powerful tool. I do not send gifts to certain clients based on their asset level or client code (except during Christmas holidays) rather, I base gifting on milestones and referrals. Always have a list of the same gifts that you use for the specific occasions. Create consistency within your practice and among your clients.

- Milestones are for clients who have reached certain ages or achieved certain goals. Examples of milestones include birthdays (16, 40, 50, 60, 70, 80, 90, 100), achievements (school graduations, retirement, etc.), and anniversaries (5, 10, 25, 50).
- Referral gifts are commonplace. How you give the gift makes all the difference. I have a nice binder with three front/back laminated pages

containing three gifts per page for a total of eighteen gifts. Each gift has a color picture and description of the gift, and all the gifts are approximately the same value. Now, when a referral from a current client comes into your office and they decide to become a client themselves at the end of the meeting pull out the gift binder.

- This part is key. Here is what you say:

  "[Mr. & Mrs. New Client], referrals are a big part of my practice. The more my clients introduce to me to their friends and family, the less time I must spend on marketing, which in turn gives me more time to focus on you and the rest of my clients. This is a huge benefit to me, and I like to show my clients that I deeply appreciate their help. Since you probably know what [referring client] would like better than I would, I'd appreciate your help you could help choose the gift that I will send them for our introduction."

- Open the binder, slide it across the table, and give your new clients a few minutes to choose the gift.

Do you see what just happened?!? You aren't just giving your client a gift for referring a new client, you are showing the new client that there are perks to referring people and showing them the nice gifts that they too can receive just for referring friends and family to your practice. How powerful a marketing technique is that?!

5. NEWSLETTER

A newsletter is an amazingly easy tool to have at your fingertips. Your current broker dealer may offer a ready-made newsletter that they will affix your picture and contact information to. At the very least take advantage of this and sign everyone you meet up for this newsletter, with their permission of course. Whether it is monthly or quarterly, a newsletter will help you stay in front of clients and prospects as the go to source for financial needs.

If you create your own newsletter, make certain that you keep the information practical for your audience. Consider that your audience may not be interested in the same things you are. The newsletter should have topics that are easily understood and enjoyable for your audience. The newsletter's format should not change from month to month because your audience will come to expect a certain structure to the newsletter and should also include your picture and contact information. Remember, the newsletter itself is your advertisement; pertinent topics should help spur clients and prospects over time to contact you sooner than they would have or keep the door open for you to contact them. A quality newsletter conveys you as a pro-active advisor who keeps your clients top of mind.

6. BIOGRAPHY

A biography is a great way to convey your expertise and experience to prospects in a practical way. Basically, it should be a "resume" for prospects. Your biography should contain a small photo of yourself (headshot of upper chest up wearing a suit), business experience, designations and degrees, community service, membership affiliations, your practice areas of focus, a paragraph or two about your philosophy for your practice, and a brief listing of personal status (married, children, activities.)

7. SPEED NETWORKING

Occasionally area Chambers of Commerce will host speed-networking events. This is a quick, non-threatening way to introduce yourself to other professionals in the area. Bring your biography and a great one-minute pitch; be sure to make it unique and not bland - an extension of your value statement. Also get everyone's contact info, even if you think they couldn't possibly help you or vice-versa send a small handwritten note with a magnetic business card afterward. By the way, thank you cards and follow up cards are never about you. Thank the person for their time, tell them it was a pleasure to meet them and let them know that you will call on them in the future. Your magnetic business card and thoughtful follow up is enough to convey your professionalism.

8. YOU ARE YOUR PRACTICE

Make your own marketing and follow up calls. I have seen firsthand how important it is to not have staff make your follow up calls or marketing calls to prospects and clients. A great financial advisor courts their prospects until they become clients, and once they become clients you continually build your relationship. I have only used staff to set appointments and confirm attendance for meetings, seminars, or events.

It is important to be continuously cultivating your personal relationship with clients as well as your professional relationship. Basically, you don't want the honeymoon to end once the prospect becomes a client. You must continuously reaffirm in the client's mind why they continue to work with you. If you do not keep this question answered it's only a matter of time before another advisor comes along and sweeps them off their feet. This doesn't just boil down to your client's rate of return on their investments. It's also about the emotional connection they have with you. A client who is personally vested in their advisor's life will feel more loyalty than if it is a strictly business relationship (hence, one of the reasons for the holiday card with your family photo.)

9. STAY IN TOUCH

Reach out to your clients at least once a month. This can be through a newsletter, meeting, phone call, etc. Anything that helps keep you top of mind. Clients want an advisor who is pro-active, but not annoying. If you call, mail, or e-mail, have something important to discuss about their accounts or applicable to their accounts.

10. CHECK YOUR SPELLING

People rarely notice when you are doing things right, but everyone notices when you mess up. This is true throughout all aspects of life. One of the easiest ways to convey this importance is too think of your daily commute. Seldom do I pay attention to good drivers; however, I most always pay attention to the bad ones! The same goes for grammar. You're a professional – there should be no reason for misspellings or run on sentences. Use spell check and re-read every e-mail or letter before they are sent to clients or prospects!

11. PRACTICE, PRACTICE, PRACTICE

I'm fond of the saying "use it or lose it". It is easy to become complacent and over-confident about your skill sets. Continuously practice sales strategies and seminars; role-play meetings with friends and co-workers; even speaking in front of a mirror or video camera can help give you invaluable feedback.

12. MOVIE SCREENING

Sponsor a local screening of a new movie that is family friendly. Host it during the day or early evening – you should be able to get a group discount where everyone also receives a drink and some popcorn or candy.

13. CLIENT APPRECIATION EVENT

This should be an annual event in which you invite most of your clients. It's a fun event where children, young adults, adults, and elders can attend. This may be a local minor or major league baseball game, movie screening in the park, or a picnic with games. This is a great way to honor your clients and their business. Make it clear that this is an appreciation event and that they can invite friends and family, and you are not holding this event to market to them.

14. MULTI-LEVEL MARKETING PARTY

There are many multi-level marketing companies with good reputations such as Mary Kay, The Pampered Chef, and Tupperware. The reason to target these local MLM reps is that many times their spouse makes a good enough income to be able to support their spouse's business. In fact, I'm sure you can count 2 or 3 people you already know to call on. Ask them to host your event while you are the sponsor. This rep could provide the venue for hosting while you provide the refreshments. Again, keep the idea focused, have a way to offset some of your costs, and provide knowledgeable advice from a professional in a specific field. Tie in a certain area of your practice with the MLM products, such as budget-friendly purchase decisions.

15. NOVELTY ITEM WITH YOUR NAME

This can be a difficult marketing tool to balance cost with effectiveness. Let me share a quick story. A friend and I were playing golf at his country club and we were walking up to the tee box when the player behind us drove up and asked if he could play through. He hit his tee shot, thanked us, and asked our names, which we gave him. He handed a golf ball to each of us and said it was a small token of his appreciation for letting him play through.

The man drove off toward his ball in the cart and we looked down at the golf ball which had this man's name, business, and contact info. We finished playing that hole and when we got to the next tee box it was a par three over a huge lake. Guess which ball I used on that hole?!? The golf ball ended up at the bottom of that lake and I have no clue who gave it to me. My point being is you should be smart when spending your hard-earned money on marketing strategies.

Instead of a "good idea" think of a smart or crafty idea. Consider handing out a packet of forget-me-not seeds at your next marketing event with your contact information on them. The prospect may never use the seeds, but it made them laugh and your ingenuity will stick with them. Be unique, stand out from the crowd and make an impression.

16. GET PUBLISHED

Nothing creates credibility faster than getting published in a newspaper or magazine. As previously discussed, some periodicals will publish your articles for free or even pay you to write articles if it fills a niche in their distribution.

17. WHAT'S MISSING IN YOUR FINANCIAL PLAN?

Be gimmicky from time to time. Think outside the box and understand that a lot of your job deals not only with sales, but with psychology. Once you understand this, marketing becomes a little easier.

18. MARKETING PAMPHLETS

When I first got into this business I walked through the front door of as many local small retail businesses I could find (restaurants, dry-cleaners, nail salons, etc.) and asked if I could put a pamphlet holder with my info in it on their counter. Guess what?

Most agreed and with 2 weeks I had 5 prospect consultations because these folks had picked up my pamphlet and read about me and my services while at those local businesses.

19. PROPER DEMOGRAPHICS RESEARCH

A great way to obtain market demographics is through contacting your local city newspaper. Usually they will have someone on staff who has a breakdown of the local zip codes and the demographics within each zip code for your targeted marketing efforts.

20. BIRTHDAY/CONGRATULATORY LUNCH

There are two great opportunities to host a lunch for your client and their coworkers. One is on their birthday. The other is during the "honeymoon" phase after becoming your client. Either way, it's quite an easy conversation to have with your client.

Explain how much you enjoy having them as a client and that you'd duplicate them if you could. To thank them for their trust and confidence in your services, offer to take them and a group of their choosing out for lunch. Don't be shy in letting them know this is a great opportunity for you to meet people JUST LIKE THEM. Your client will know exactly what you mean and will be your advocate. Keep the lunch casual, letting the guests know what you do for a living, but then keeping the rest of the meal non-business related. Don't worry, your clients will do the selling for you so that when you follow up with the guests, they'll be ready to meet.

21. PRIVATE DINING

This is intimate – you, a client, and one or two of their guests. I always use the same restaurant and try to keep the same waiter. Get to the restaurant early and explain to your waiter what will be going on and the need for great service without being intrusive. Give your waiter a tip, up front.

As with any private dinner, be light yet professional. Let the conversations center around your client and their guest(s). If your client or any guest steers the conversation toward your occupation, give your value statement then politely let them know you like to keep business at the office and that you'll be following up with them anyway.

The next day, send a handwritten note to both your client and their guest(s). Included with this note should be a magnetic business card and the group photo you had your waiter take toward the end of the meal.

22. TREASURE BOX

How cool was it when you were a kid to visit the bank and get a sucker; or visit the dentist/doctor and pick out a toy from the treasure chest? Clients will sometimes bring their children or grandchildren and it is a nice touch to make sure to be thoughtful enough to please the kids when your clients come in for a visit. Fill it with toys that have your contact info on them like suggested in #15. Toy airplanes, balsa-wood airplanes, bouncy balls, mini-Frisbees, stuffed animals, notebooks, stress balls, puzzles, etc. Who knows, maybe even your client would like a toy.

23. GOLF LESSONS

This is a great opportunity for marketing as a client bring-a-friend event. Make this a memorable experience for your clients and their guest(s) by paying for a group lesson which includes a swing analysis video, putting and chipping lesson, and lunch. Get multiple group and individual photos you, your guests, and the instructor.

This is not just a typical day out on the course, and you will be able to suggest to each individual client and their guest that you should play golf together the next week. This way you get to see the prospect twice and have twice the interaction.

24. GOLF OUTING

This is the traditional day out on the course and should be intimate with no more than four players, including yourself. I recommend scheduling tee times in the early afternoon so the group can enjoy a drink or two in the clubhouse afterward. When scheduling the golf round be sure to tell the clubhouse what you are doing and ask for their help in making this a special outing. They should be more than happy to help accommodate since this is also a marketing opportunity for them!

Schedule enough time so your guests can practice on the driving range and putting green before the round begins. Afterwards, have someone from the clubhouse take a group photo.

As with most other marketing activities, follow up with a handwritten note, magnetic business card, and your group photo.

25. CASINO NIGHT

This can be tricky to pull off and have can have many people attend. It helps if you have partners or other advisors go in on this as a group marketing event. Team up with a local charity to see if they will provide dealers for the tables and volunteers for the event. The proceeds should always go to benefit this charity and offset some of your costs.

Attendees pay a certain amount to get in the door and are given a set number of "betting chips". Prizes are awarded to those with the most chips, or you can hold a silent auction (be sure to check state and local laws.) If the proceeds are for charity – you can sometimes find free advertising available in local newspapers. Also, it's ok to start small and build in size and attendance year after year, growing sponsorship and conversion.

26. WINE TASTING

Contact local wineries, if available, or wine stores. Most likely they already have wine tasting events on their books. Offer to cover a certain amount of their costs and in exchange you are listed as a host or sponsor.

Inform the business that you'll be inviting your clients and guests to increase their exposure as well (win-win). This cross-pollination of clients is exactly what EVERY business wants, and you are happy to help!

Another idea is to have an auction where each attendee receives a ticket. You should pay for the auction item(s), announce the drawing and winner(s). Included in the auction item(s) should be a handwritten congratulatory card and your magnetic business card.

27. COOKING CLASS

Many local culinary teaching facilities offer group events. Much like some of the other marketing strategies, reach out and offer to co-host their event. The business should have a great venue, good reputation, and knowledgeable professionals. Keep your idea focused, offset some of the costs, and have a gift from the hosting business to give each of your attendees. And, you guessed it, follow up with a handwritten note, magnetic business card, and your group photo.

28. RETIREMENT PARTY

This is a fantastic way to show your own appreciation for your client and let them know that you were an integral part of their retirement planning process. Consider having 3 different options for venue and theme so that you can have a turn-key process while still making it unique for your clients.

Ultimately, this should be a fun and memorable event; and the details do make a big difference. Fun invitations, framed photos of the client's life in & out of the work environment, games, music, finger-foods, it's up to you to make it light and fun how you want. This should not be an expensive event for you – remember that it is all about creating an opportunity for your client to be celebrated. If done right, the client will feel a full range of emotions and connect those great feelings to you.

29. SPA DAY

Work with a local day spa and try to have them co-op the event because you will be providing them with a great marketing event and exposure to new potential clients. As with most intimate events, I limit the number of attendees. Invite a client and have them bring 2 – 4 friends or invite two clients and have them invite 1 – 2 friends. Discuss package options with the spa and create a memorable event with champagne and chocolates.

30. ART SHOWS

An Art Show event should be conducted the same as a wine tasting. Not only will your clients and prospects be there, but also many other attendees to meet! It's important to invite clients who've already expressed interest in the arts and that have friends who are interested as well. You can have a flawless event, but if the clients and prospects who attend do not appreciate the atmosphere, then this could be a waste of time and money.

31. DEEP SEA / LAKE FISHING

This event can be enjoyed by men and women; however, it is somewhat more involved to plan. A fishing expedition should be more intimate and involve one or two clients and their guests (your prospects.)

32. HEALTH & WEALTH SCREENING

Partner with a local medical professional such as an optometrist, chiropractor, or podiatrist and offer a complimentary specialty health screening and financial health screening. This is a great way for both you and the medical professional to split costs and promote your practices.

33. SCRAPBOOK EVENT

This is a great event for people of all ages. Find a local Arts and Crafts or Scrapbooking store and ask them to co-host your event while you sponsor. The store will have a great venue for hosting, a knowledgeable professional and plenty of supplies. At most you could cover half the cost of supplies and refreshments. Again, keep the idea focused, have a way to offset some of your costs, and provide knowledgeable advice from a professional in that field.

34. BECOME A SPONSOR

Imagine your logo on banners at fundraisers, charity events, or at local high school football games. Money spent on promotions involving non-profits or in the community is money well-spent. You will be able to generate an immediately positive appearance. The key is consistency and saturation.

35. TARGETED SEMINAR SERIES

As mentioned before, it is quite easy to find inexpensive ways to hold seminars, but one of the most overlooked areas is within your own church. Talk to your board of elders, priest, or preacher and offer to host a 3/4/6-week series on Bible-based money management or even something unrelated to biblical teachings such as college education or estate planning. You will be able to "advertise" in your local church and news bulletins and be top of mind for your entire congregation.

36. VIDEOCONFERENCE

These are simple to carry out and can be a huge asset to your practice. This is a great way to stay top of mind with current clients by providing excellent value and a perfect way to establish trust and set yourself apart from the competition with prospects.

Put your teleseminars on a set schedule – this will be easier for you and your attendees. Your topics should be engaging and easy to understand and tailored for the specific audience you invite.

37. VIDEO BLOG

Like teleseminars these are simple to carry out and can help establish instant trust and credibility with prospects while also deepening client relationships. This can be a monthly three to five-minute video where you discuss the current economic environment, new tax laws, or any other pertinent financial topic. Hosting can be done for free at several websites, and once you finish you could e-mail the link or actual video to your clients and prospects. Use engaging topic titles and key points that will help convince the audience to watch.

38. CLIENT MEETINGS VIA VIDEOCONFERENCE

Believe it or not, there are quite a few clients who would rather not come in for annual or semi-annual meetings. Especially during the COVID-19 Global Pandemic of 2020!

Outside of a global stay-at-home order, many of my clients are busy professionals and trying to nail down a time for them to come to my office for a one-hour meeting is like trying to nail jello to a wall – not gonna happen.

Another option is to host a meeting through the internet. Research internet meeting hosting sites and find the most secure option to be able to show presentations and portfolio updates. Before assuming your clients would like this choice, give them the option.

39. ADVERTISE IN CREATIVE PLACES

Most people think of advertising on a billboard or in the newspaper. Get those creative juices flowing and think about where your target market frequents. If you are targeting a large attorney firm find out where they eat lunch a lot and see if you can sponsor the restaurant's menu or host a free lunch giveaway that patrons can enter when they come for lunch where you pick up the tab and introduce yourself.

40. PLAY GOLF/TENNIS BY YOURSELF

This is a fantastic way to meet new people! Just walk on up to the course/court and get on as a single – this can work at a public, semi-public, or private (if you're a member.) Or, if you plan on playing at that location regularly, talk it up with the pros behind the counter. They could keep an open window for you at a specific time every week.

Once you get on the course or on the court, talk to the people you've been teamed up with about what they do for a living. Eventually they will ask you what you do and that's when you give your value statement and shut up. Play the rest of the round/game building great rapport and then you can do one of two things.

Tell the other players that it was a pleasure meeting them and offer to exchange business cards and go on your way.

OR

Ask them if they have time for a drink (if they say no, you can still exchange cards.) The secret to having an effective post-game drink is to only have one drink, make a good impression, pay for everyone's drinks, and leave. A good rule of thumb in any situation is to leave them wanting more. If you really want to start establishing quality prospects at the local clubhouse, make friends with the bartenders. Tip them well – make sure they know your name, what you like to drink, what you do, and make sure they have a great impression of you. Most people like and trust the bartenders who work at golf/tennis clubs and value their opinions on other people.

41. COMPLIMENTARY CONSULTATION PRIZE

Offer a free financial consultation as a prize in local charity events, giveaways, business promotions, etc.

42. TESTIMONIALS

This could be a great addition to any marketing piece you have. Talk to your top clients and discuss how you would like to use a testimony from them to promote your practice. Ask them if they would draft a letter, in their own words, describing your practice and the positive experience they have working with you. Be sure to get their permission to reprint their testimony. Anytime a prospect can read about someone else's positive experience with you may help push that prospect to act. (Be aware of applicable rules & regulations.)

43. TEACH

Give a speech or volunteer for a career day at local colleges and graduate schools. Getting in front of the next generation of professionals and then signing them up for your newsletter will help provide a stream of prospects for the future. Another idea is to discuss teaching a class at the local colleges or adult education centers on personal finance issues. Again, it is important to constantly be in front of people; and what better way to market than by giving back to the community at the same time!

44. INTRODUCE YOURSELF TO BUSINESS OWNERS

The idea behind this is as old as sales. Pick an area of your city, or a small "main street" town, and spend the day walking into as many businesses you can. Your goal is to meet either the manager or the owner. This is not the time to be aggressive – this is only a factfinding mission. Let the owner/manager know who you are and what you do. Tell them that you're hitting the streets to meet new people, learn about their business, and see if there are opportunities where you may be able to provide help. Remember that you are a business owner and business owners will appreciate your fearlessness and determination.

45. PICK UP THE PHONE

A day shouldn't go by that you aren't speaking with a prospect face to face or over the phone. You can't sit back and wait for the perfect scenario. If a prospect is going to say no, then get it out of the way and move on! There are too many potential prospects out there for you to not try and move on. Make your calls brief. Don't try to sell the client over the phone. Your goal should be to get the appointment, not sell a product!

46. BUILD RELATIONSHIPS WITH LOCAL AUTO DEALERS

If you sell auto insurance, you should be building relationships today with local new and used auto dealerships. Remember, people don't necessarily promote other businesses unless they have some skin in the game, so offer incentives to these salespeople to pass out your pamphlet to auto buyers. Incentives can include gift certificates, monthly prizes for the most referrals, whatever you think of that will be approved by your compliance department.

47. CONTINUE MARKETING UP

Just because someone comes to you with one particular need, don't assume that they won't benefit from another product or service you offer. Continue offering your full suite of services. I worked with a client for a full year managing their insurance needs before they trusted me enough to discuss the quarter of a million dollars in an old retirement plan from a company they left two years before coming to me for insurance solutions.

48. BUY LUNCH

Put your ego aside and check your nerves at the door! This one can be a little daunting but could bring instant reward. Go to a local restaurant and find a table with professionals eating lunch. Politely interrupt and let them know you're a local financial advisor and if they'll allow you five minutes to speak, you'll buy their lunches. Have a planned script and book some appointments!

49. BE PROFESSIONAL

This is often an overlooked aspect of marketing, but one of the most important. You do not want to be a distraction to your prospects and clients. The simplest way to achieving trust and respect is to dress appropriately for your position. As a financial services representative it is important that you have a firm handshake - do not confuse firm with tight. Ensure that perfume or cologne is not overpowering. A former co-worker of mine blew a deal because the prospect he met with was allergic to his cologne! Wear outfits that do not draw attention to yourself; when in doubt wear a blue or white shirt, pay attention to nails, accessories, shoes, and grooming. And most importantly, maintain proper eye contact (no stare-downs – let your eyes show your compassion and warmth, not intimidation).

50. DON'T STOP MARKETING AND DON'T GIVE UP!!!

Do you feel like you got cheated on #50? Well, you didn't. You just haven't needed to use this one yet!

51. FISHBOWLS (YEP, I GAVE YOU AN EXTRA ONE)

When I started my career, part of my first year's growth came from taking groups of people to lunch two or three days a week. Here's how it works:

- Choose restaurants in your city that offer a mid-priced lunch and are generally busy during lunchtime.

- Take a day and go to each of those restaurants, speak to the owner/manager about generating some more business for them by adding a "free lunch" bowl near their cash register or host stand. The purpose is to generate interest in your services and in return you'll hold at least one lunch every week where you'll bring up to ten people to their restaurant.

- You'll want anywhere from five to ten restaurants that agree to this to make it worthwhile.

- Buy your plastic fishbowls, add a placard which has your logo and says, "Place your business card in the bowl for a chance to win a complimentary lunch." When you drop off your bowls, be sure to reengage the owner/manager and get their buy-in again and let them know that you'll be by once a week to pick up the cards.

- The key is that every card dropped in the bowl is a winner! Call everyone, introduce yourself and be enthusiastic about the person winning that week's drawing:

  > *Hi, may I speak with [name].*
  > *Hello, [name], my name is [your name].*
  > *Recently you dropped your business card for a chance to win a complimentary lunch at [restaurant]. I'm happy to let you know that you won this week's drawing! Congratulations! Let me explain how this works. To get my name out in the community, I sponsor one*

lunch a week for you and up to five other people of your choosing to have lunch at [restaurant name]. When you and your guests arrive, I'll introduce myself, give a brief five-minute presentation about my services as a financial advisor, and then leave you and your guests to enjoy your complimentary lunch.

Now, the days I have set aside for these lunches are Tuesdays and Thursdays @ 11:30. What day is best for you?

- Now that you've set the lunch there are a couple other things to be mindful of:

    Arrive a few minutes early to speak to your waiter/waitress. You'll want them to have your card on file so that you can just leave after you're finished speaking to your group and your card can just be billed.

    Get straight to the script – your script should be about who you are, what areas of financial planning you help your clients and a call to action.

    After your finished, ask if there are any questions.

    After answering any questions, pass around an evaluation form – explain that you must collect personal info since this is a form of marketing but that they can request to not be contacted OR if they have any questions to mark it on the form.

Once they've completed the form and passed them back to you, get the group to lean in for a photo that you'll take and email them later that day or week.

The next morning, email the photo, and then that afternoon call the prospects who gave you permission to discuss their concerns and book a formal meeting.

CHAPTER 5 - PROSPECTS & MEETINGS

Alright, you have done the toughest thing – you have created a prospect, now what? There may be some questions/concerns going through your mind.

- How soon should I call them?
- What if our personalities don't match?
- What if they say no?
- What do I do if they ask me a question I don't know?

Here's my advice: Calm Down! You can't control the outcome of situations. You will get NO's. You will offend people. You will be asked questions that you've never heard. Do you think that the people who make it in this industry defy all the statistics and never get a NO? Do you think that the people who succeed in this business never get hung up on? C'mon, take a deep breath and get those silly thoughts out of your head – you already know the answers! The difference between people who succeed in this industry and those that don't is desire and determination.

SETTING THE APPOINTMENT

Let's discuss effective phone or face to face conversations to set an appointment with a prospect. First, always set a meeting with a prospect as soon as possible. You want their need for a financial advisor to be fresh on their mind when they sit down with you. The latest I ever booked an appointment and had it hold was two weeks. For that simple reason I make sure that all prospect meetings are booked within two weeks of my conversation – any farther out than that, either your prospect isn't serious, and you should not take them serious or you did not build up sufficient concern for them to want to take action. If they are not serious move on to the next prospect; if you were unable to engage them, rethink your approach with your prospects.

All conversations with prospects should center around them, not you. A great financial advisor is constantly asking open-ended questions such as:

- What is most important to you right now?
- Why has this become a concern for you?
- What would you like to see happen?
- Tell me more about that.

Remember that people enjoy talking about themselves and generally have a positive view of people who will listen. Anyone can tell a prospect, "My financial advisory practice focuses on a personal relationship with my clients helping them achieve their financial goals by providing individual solutions to meet those goals." Sounds great to you, but all your prospect hears is "Blah, Blah, Blah."

What you say isn't what separates you from the competition. It's how you listen that helps you stand out from the thousands of other advisors out there. A skilled financial advisor leads their prospects down a path which allows the prospect to express the need to come sit down with you. This is a whole lot easier than most people think. It requires a little bit of self-restrain and control at first but should become natural over time. Keep tension on the conversation by asking the open-ended questions. Whether it is insurance, investments, estate planning, there's usually a "hot button" that a prospect has strong emotional ties to right now. Find that "hot button" using the above-mentioned questions and be sure to have them talk a little in depth about their financial goals or concerns, then follow these simple steps to build concern:

Hot Button	*"What are you currently doing about...?"*
Goal	*"What would you like to accomplish with...?"*
Obstacle	*"What do you see getting in the way of accomplishing...?"*
Consequence	*"How would you feel if... (tie back to the obstacle)?"*

In doing this, you are providing the valid and necessary questions to help a prospect realize that they need your help. When they were answering your questions and discussing their goals, etc. your answer to everything should be brief, such as *"hmm"* or *"I see."* In these instances, less is more.

Do not offer answers and do not tell the prospect that they are okay or that they are doing a good job. Don't focus on trying to be liked by your prospects. You could end up falsely validating that the prospect does not need your help!

After you have the prospect realizing that they need your help, it is time to take it away. This builds urgency on top of the concern. Your closing to the conversation should go something like this:

"It sounds like your main priorities are …. And your greatest concerns are…."
"What has prevented you from putting together a plan to reach these goals?"
<PAUSE & LISTEN>
"Mr./Mrs. Prospect, based on what you've told me, I recommend that we sit down for an hour to see how I can help you. My initial consultations are complimentary and will help us determine two things:
Whether or not you need my help, and
Whether or not I will bring you into my practice."
<PAUSE BRIEFLY>
"What does your schedule look like at the end of this week?"

This is a powerful closing statement. It shows your prospect that you are selective with your clients. If a prospect doesn't seem concerned about their financial issues or appears skeptical of you, then I'd suggest politely telling them that they would be better off discussing their financial priorities with someone else. I've found these clients take up too much of your time and one day could end up being a liability for your practice.

SIX CHARACTERISTICS & BEHAVIORS WHEN CALLING PROSPECTS

- Convey Confidence & Positivity
- Match Prospect's Tone & Pace
- Stick to Your Script – Stay Consistent
- Show Empathy
- Listen Effectively
- Expand on Prospect's Goals & Concerns

PROSPECT APPOINTMENT MISTAKES TO AVOID

- Stay away from addressing your prospects as Mr./Mrs. Use first names, it's more intimate and leads to a deeper connection.
- Do not repeat negative responses, i.e., *"So you're not interested in mutual funds?"*

- Do not ask, *"Is your husband/wife available?"* Don't assume who makes the financial decisions for the household. See #1.
- If you leave a message a voicemail, be vague. This is not to be deceitful, but to encourage interest.
- Do not discuss products or solutions and don't get caught defending or denigrating products or companies. Instead, tell them something along the lines of, *"Different solutions make sense for different people. Once I understand your financial needs, we will work together to find the most cost-efficient and effective way to reach your goals given your own personal circumstance."*
- Do not expect a positive conversation for the first couple minutes until you're able to establish commonality and rapport.
- Do not request that detailed information be prepared before your first meeting. Instead tell them that having certain information with them will be helpful, but not necessary. Minimize roadblocks to holding an appointment.
- Do not try to make friends with the prospect over the phone. Find a similar commonality, such as last night's thunderstorm, to establish rapport and then get to the script.
- Never prove the prospect wrong – on anything – period! If you need to answer, *"That*

sounds interesting – we can discuss that in more detail when we meet."

- Steer clear of interrogative questions, i.e., *"Do you invest in mutual funds?"* Instead, use open-ended questions/statements such as, *"Tell me about your current investments."*
- The tone of your voice and how well you listen carry a much bigger impact than the actual words that you speak.
- Be sure to confirm your address along with the prospect's physical and e-mail address.
- Never get angry or upset over the phone. Maintain control – stay in charge.
- Don't be intimidated. Many times, prospects will express that they already work with a financial professional – learn to take this in stride and continue setting an appointment.
- Do ask if their spouse will be available for the meeting (if applicable).
- Use open-ended questions.
- Remember to find and expand upon the prospect's "hot buttonLearn" to pick up on clues. When a prospect convinces themselves that they need to see you there should be verbal clues, such as *"what are your office hours?"* or *"how does this work?"* As soon as you pick up on these clues move straight to setting an appointment!
- Do not be pushy.
- Pick up the phone!

VOICEMAIL

- Call your lead twice a week, but only leave one message per week. A quality message from you can convey a personal touch that e-mails, and direct mails do not. This is usually your first or second level of contact, so it is important to leave a message.
- After introducing yourself, always re-establish you connection with that person.
- When leaving your message be upbeat but not too excited – you don't want to come across as a trying to sell someone a product. Be short and to the point. When someone listens to a message, they immediately formulate a "mental" image of you by your tone, speed, context, and confidence.
- Your message should never say, *"If you have any questions, you can call me back."* Or, *"If you feel like it would be a good idea to talk, you can reach me at…"* No one will call you back! Rather, be assumptive that they want to call back by saying, *"I look forward to hearing back from you soon. I will call you back at the end of the week if we haven't been able to talk."*
- Be extremely confident in your message and that your prospect should call you back.
- Every lead is valuable and as such your goal is to get some sort of decision from the prospect – a yes or a no.

CHAPTER 6 – CONCLUSION

This guide is just that, a guide. Much like following a map to reach your destination, you can choose to take the most direct route in the least amount of time, or you could choose other potential routes. Either way, you MUST keep moving forward. As long as you don't let roadblocks, detours or unexpected delays deter you from reaching your destination you will eventually arrive.

I can't stress the importance of momentum enough in this career. It requires great emotional strength to weather the ups and downs you'll face – remember the Cardinal Rule in prospecting:

PEOPLE DON'T REJECT OTHER PEOPLE, THEY JUST REJECT THE TIMING

We never know what other people are going through in their personal or professional life and just because a person doesn't need your expertise today doesn't mean they won't need it next month or next year. The longer you're in this business the more you'll see that prospects who said "no" to you previously may be receptive to your calls and conversations today. The emotional rollercoaster can be difficult to handle if you let those emotions dictate your thoughts and actions. Which is why I highly recommend finding a mentor.

A mentor is someone with the expertise to help develop your career. This may sound broad and so it is up to you to determine what type of relationship you'll need to be successful. A good mentor should provide balanced advice to help build your professional development and be a role model who listens to your fears and frustrations while helping re-focus your energy and enthusiasm.

Your mentor does not have to be another financial advisor. So, take time to consider what it is you need in a mentor. Are you looking for someone who'll help guide your marketing efforts? Are you looking for someone who can listen to your ongoing fears and emotions so you're able to release those feelings and move on? Is it someone who can give you guidance and advice on specific aspects of your career? Regardless, your mentor-mentee relationship should have structure and clear expectations, if not, then it will be a waste of time. And time is something you cannot afford to lose this early in your career.

Consider a family friend, a life-coach, or an internet search to find the right mentor who fits with your personality, expectations, and ethics. FPA Connect offers MentorMatch, connecting financial advisors together as mentor/mentee relationships. When choosing another advisor to be your mentor, it can be easy to focus on what that advisor's practice looks like now. However, you weren't around for the years of hard work and sacrifices that person went through to be where they are today. Use your time and relationship with your mentor to focus on the processes which will make you successful.

This book and the tools that accompany it should be a guide for you much the same as a mentor. Refer to these tools, tips, and strategies regularly while you build your practice and your brand. Your long-term success is dependent on so many things that it can be easy to think you need to "re-create the wheel" and spend time building new scripts, marketing activities, etc. Please do not fall into this trap – you'll be mistaking activity for achievement.

Over time, you'll find that certain strategies work best for you and some do not. This is because we are all unique in our abilities, limitations, and communication styles. The fact that you're reading this means you have the drive and desire to succeed. Believe in yourself. You are in a unique opportunity to impact not just your own future, but the future of every one of your clients and the generations of family to follow them.

TRUST YOURSELF.
TRUST THE PROCESS.
BECAUSE YOU NOW HAVE THE
SECRETS
OF
SUCCESS